T0323607

Cambridge Elements ≡

Elements in Religion and Monotheism
edited by
Paul K. Moser
Loyola University Chicago
Chad Meister
*Affiliate Scholar, Ansari Institute for Global Engagement with Religion,
University of Notre Dame*

MUSIC AND MONOTHEISM

Gareth F. Wilson
University of Cambridge

Shaftesbury Road, Cambridge CB2 8EA, United Kingdom

One Liberty Plaza, 20th Floor, New York, NY 10006, USA

477 Williamstown Road, Port Melbourne, VIC 3207, Australia

314–321, 3rd Floor, Plot 3, Splendor Forum, Jasola District Centre, New Delhi – 110025, India

103 Penang Road, #05–06/07, Visioncrest Commercial, Singapore 238467

Cambridge University Press is part of Cambridge University Press & Assessment, a department of the University of Cambridge.

We share the University's mission to contribute to society through the pursuit of education, learning and research at the highest international levels of excellence.

www.cambridge.org
Information on this title: www.cambridge.org/9781009158923

DOI: 10.1017/9781009158916

First published 2024

A catalogue record for this publication is available from the British Library

ISBN 978-1-009-51704-1 Hardback
ISBN 978-1-009-15892-3 Paperback
ISSN 2631-3014 (online)
ISSN 2631-3006 (print)

Music and Monotheism

Elements in Religion and Monotheism

DOI: 10.1017/9781009158916
First published online: November 2024

Gareth F. Wilson
University of Cambridge

Author for correspondence: Gareth F. Wilson, nota1cambiata@hotmail.com

Abstract: What connects the phenomenon of music as an art with the belief in one indivisible God? What has music, a non-linguistic medium, to say about the personal, loving, communicative God of Scripture and the Prophets, or the omniscient, omnipotent, omnipresent, transcendent God of the philosophers and can it bring these 'concepts of God' together? To answer these questions, this Element takes divine Creation as its starting point, that the God of monotheism must be the Creator of all that is. It thus argues that anything that instantiates and facilitates communication within the created realm has been enabled to do so by a God who communicates with His creation, and who wishes that His creation be communicative. Indeed, it will argue that the communication allowed by music, and aesthetic experience in general, is the very raison d'être of Abrahamic monotheism and might thus allow an opportunity for dialogue between monotheistic faiths.

This element also has a video abstract: www.cambridge.org/Wilson

Keywords: music, theology, aesthetics, communicability, creation

ISBNs: 9781009517041 (HB), 9781009158923 (PB), 9781009158916 (OC)
ISSNs: 2631-3014 (online), 2631-3006 (print)

Contents

1 Introduction

An eminent composer once visited a prestigious university music department to deliver a lecture on the opera *Wozzeck* by the Austrian/Jewish composer Alban Berg. After playing a short instrumental extract from the piece, he asked each person present to summarise in one word what they thought the music communicated and was both surprised and dismayed when he received no fewer than thirteen different answers. Why thirteen? Because the lecture was attended by thirteen people, each of whose response to the music seemed valid, although many answers were mutually exclusive and none matched what the lecturer believed Berg was trying to convey.

The exercise provides a salient lesson to anyone who chooses to write about music, regardless of the context: music and conceptual language work in different ways because they do not share the same purpose. The assumption of the *Wozzeck* exercise was that the music would communicate a concept immediately comprehensible to all who were present, that each would understand exactly the same thing. But music does *not* communicate concepts and, because no two people are the same, each will bring a different framework of interpretation (their mood, personal taste, listening experience, their history, their very selves) to the experience of listening to it. All of this means that the *Wozzeck* experiment, however well-meaning, was always doomed to failure.

This is why I have never been comfortable reading or listening to commentaries on music, on what the music is purported to say or do, partly because this does not speak to my experience of listening to or making music, and partly because I feel it does an injustice to music as a communicative medium, presupposing that music is insufficiently communicative on its own and requires an interpreter to explain its 'intentions' in other ways. Even when the composer provides his or her own explanation (or programme note) for what their music means I have always sensed an incongruence for the reasons demonstrated by the *Wozzeck* experiment. And, although I am interested in what others might have to say about a piece of music, I do not require them, or even the composer, to interpret on my behalf and believe that their attempts to do so must necessarily fall short of what music most powerfully does when left to communicate on its own terms with its listeners.

While this might come across as excessively individualistic, I hope to demonstrate in this short enquiry that isolationism is not the *telos* of my argument. Instead, what I am trying to do is lay the groundwork for a theology of music which might find purchase in traditions other than my own thereby suggesting a possible avenue for an interreligious dialogue which is less dependent on discursive argument and more based upon shared experience.

To explain, I am a Christian and a practising 'Classical' musician, active in the performance, composition, and teaching of what is currently referred to as Western Art Music. I do this within liturgical, concert, and educational contexts. I have worked for more than twenty years as a liturgical Director of Music in the Anglican tradition both in churches and in university chapels and have extensive experience of Roman Catholic worship although my religious background originates in the Church of Scotland wherein I occasionally worship today. My formal theological training has been undertaken by Jesuit priests, Anglican theologians, and atheist philosophers. Some might see this as an eclectic and wide-ranging background but in the face of a project on Music and Monotheism I consider it impossibly limited. I have no right to dictate to Jews, Muslims, Sikhs, or even other Christians what I think their conception of music ought to be nor have I the space or knowledge to enumerate the vast range of musical practices which these traditions employ. I could not even presume to be able to do this with the Christian religion. What I seek to do, then, is carve out a niche within which music can be talked about which might find common ground between radically different traditions and cultures without underplaying these differences and creating offense. I am painfully aware that to speak from one perspective and suggest that other traditions simply find their own way will come off as unacceptably dismissive and uninterested in other cultures. I hope to show that that is not the case. But I am also conscious of how unpopular it now is to claim that music is a universal language, that to many this smacks of cultural imperialism, assumes the superiority of one particular type of music (i.e., the very type of music that I usually practise), and ignores a history of musical colonialism. And yet, while not wishing to be dismissive of these concerns, I cannot ignore a nagging urge to argue that music *does* enjoy a certain universality, and it will be on the basis of this claim that I hope to provide the interreligious avenue to which I previously alluded. It is hoped that those who are made nervous by this comment will come to realise that I do not quite mean it in the same way that it has sometimes been made in the past,[1] but

---

[1] In *Nineteenth-Century Music*, Carl Dahlhaus reports that '[. . .] in its basic features, compositional technique remained universal until Debussy's inconspicuous and Schoenberg's spectacular musical revolutions', and later writes that '[. . .] the audience for whom Beethoven wrote his symphonies was nothing less than "humanity," in the dual sense of an all-embracing throng and a substance which, however buried in convention, was common to all people'. C. Dahlhaus, *Nineteenth-Century Music*, tr. J. Bradford Robinson (Los Angeles & London: University of California Press, 1989), pp. 35–36. Whether these comments are intended to reflect attitudes of the long nineteenth-century or more recent times, musicologists today would be wary of their Eurocentrism. As the arguments of this enquiry evolve, it will be clear that I do not presume to dictate which musics should be enjoyed by which people. But while I acknowledge the context that Dahlhaus is specifically writing about Western Art Music here, it is important to recognise that there is not, and never has been, a 'universal' compositional technique.

I will also strive to provide sufficient theological support from my own experience in order to justify the approach to music that I will offer in these pages. If nothing else, I hope that what is written here will encourage readers to reflect upon what their own relationship to music might be, and to consider this relationship in light of their own faith or belief system. Put differently, what does it *mean* to have a relationship with something like music, how does any form of religious faith condition this relationship, and where would our faith be without it?

1.1 Methodology

Having already claimed that music is not a conceptual medium, and that language about music can never do it justice, I should clarify that I am arguing not so much about music but about the significance of my inability to write about it.[2] Specifically, my concern is to explore not the performing or composing of music but the *affective experience* of simply listening to it.[3] What is the *meaningfulness* of said experience and, for the purposes of interreligious dialogue, what is the significance of a shared capacity for aesthetic enjoyment across differing faith-based, or cultural, contexts? My wrestling with these questions will therefore owe more to philosophical theology than to musicological analysis. With two exceptions, I will not analyse particular pieces of music and try to derive a theological message from them. Unless the music has been specifically composed in such a way as to invite that type of investigation I believe this approach damages music by putting words into its mouth thereby diminishing its inherent communicative power and potential;[4] the *Wozzeck* experiment mentioned earlier stimulated a large number of differing (and intriguing) interpretations but might not have done so had we been told in

---

[2] *Pace* Jeremy Begbie, Nicholas Cook, Berthold Hoeckner, Martha Nussbaum, and Roger Scruton among others, claiming that we cannot speak or write about music and having a lot to say about this inability are quite different things. The inability is philosophically, theologically, and existentially significant, and it is right that we should explore its ramifications. Doing so does not mean that the language we use about music has much meaningful purchase – my contention remains that it does not, cf. J. Begbie, *Music, Modernity, and God: Essays in Easy Listening* (Oxford: Oxford University Press, 2013) p. 187; N. Cook, *Analysing Musical Multimedia* (Oxford: Clarendon Press, 1998), pp. 266–267; B. Hoeckner, *Programming the Absolute: Nineteenth-Century German Music and the Hermeneutics of the Moment* (Princeton & Oxford: Princeton University Press, 2002) pp.3–4; M. Nussbaum, *Upheavals of Thought: The Intelligence of Emotions* (Cambridge: Cambridge University Press, 2001), p.255; Roger Scruton, 'Effing the Ineffable', Effing the Ineffable – Sir Roger Scruton (roger-scruton.com) accessed 12/04/2023.

[3] I would like to add, however, that the 'affective level' is also central to the composition and performing of music.

[4] I will offer one example where I believe such an approach is musically and theologically justifiable although the credit for this belongs to the composer, not the analyst. However, much that is theologically instructive can sometimes be gained by attempts at this which are *unsuccessful*. I shall offer two such examples of this.

advance what we were expected to hear. My hope, however, is not simply to offer a *paean* to music's ineffability, but to demonstrate the theological value of said ineffability as well as to illustrate its relevance within the context of monotheism. Indeed, I will argue that monotheism itself demands that theology recognise and utilise music's 'unsayability' not just for the purposes of academic discussion but for the praxis of worship and the daily journey of faith.

I also cannot attempt to offer a survey of the different varieties of music employed by the monotheistic faiths, not only because to do so properly would require several volumes and the collaboration of numerous experts from every field, but because I do not believe that doing so would add anything to the types of theological arguments I am trying to make.[5] The fact that there *is* such a vast range of human creativity, religiously inspired or otherwise, is in and of itself of tremendous theological significance, of course, and may say something about our being created in the image of the divine Creator, but to delve into specific musics will have to remain a project for another time. Also, for reasons of conciseness, I will restrict the discussion to the Abrahamic religions of Judaism, Christianity, and Islam (or 'Abrahamic monotheism').

If it is surprising that a theologically-oriented discussion on music and monotheism can take us into doctrinal territory stretching to Creation, revelation, grace, election, fallenness, as well as language, meaningfulness, and morality then all the better, but the questions I ask in this enquiry will remain as questions. My intention is to demonstrate that they deserve to be asked; while own views may easily be inferred I am more interested in the openness of this discussion and identifying the directions in which it might point than in arriving at any sense of finality or neat resolution.

2 Arnold Schoenberg – *Moses und Aron*

Having concluded that human suffering was beyond endurance, a certain Rebbe went up to heaven and knocked at the Messiah's gate. 'Why are you taking so long?' he asked him. 'Don't you know mankind is expecting you?' 'It's not me they

---

[5] The three pieces of music I discuss, by J. S. Bach, Ludwig van Beethoven, and Arnold Schoenberg, respectively, come from the Western Classical tradition. While some might object to this within the context of a purported attempt at interreligious dialogue, I would respond that these pieces have been chosen, first, because they are explicitly concerned with the question of God, second, because they are concerned with asking an important theological question about a purported separability between God and Creation which is relevant to the three religions in question and is one of the central themes this text seeks to address, and third, because they belong to the type of music about which I am qualified to offer original insights; while an attempt to include musics from other cultures and traditions might appear more inclusive, I would feel uncomfortable making musical observations which are not sufficiently informed by life-experience and a strong sense of personal ownership. I therefore hope that my choosing a path of caution might be inferred as a mark of respect rather than one of dismissiveness.

are expecting,' answered the Messiah. 'Some are waiting for good health and riches. Others for serenity and knowledge. Or peace in the home and happiness. No, it's not me they are awaiting.'

At this point, they say, the Rebbe lost patience and cried: 'So be it! If you have but one face, may it remain in shadow! If you cannot help men, all men, resolve their problems, all their problems, even the most insignificant, then stay where you are, as you are. If you still have not guessed that you are bread for the hungry, a voice for the old man without heirs, sleep for those who dread night, if you have not understood all this and more: that every wait is a wait for you, then you are telling the truth: indeed, it is not you that mankind is waiting for.'

The Rebbe came back to earth, gathered his disciples and forbade them to despair:

'And now the true waiting begins.'

The True Waiting (Elie Wiesel)

As a starting point I shall take the opera *Moses und Aron* by the Austrian composer, Arnold Schoenberg (1874–1951), an opera driven by the very question of God, of how the divine should be understood, and of how His presence should be communicated. It focuses upon the revelation of the Ten Commandments at Sinai and the incident of the Golden Calf and is therefore a narrative which speaks to Judaism, Christianity, and Islam and is a foundational moment within Abrahamic monotheism. And while Schoenberg's take on the narrative is a particularly Jewish one (although some claim that the Moses presented is not the Moses of Scripture but is Schoenberg's own conception),[6] the issues raised by a discussion of this opera go to the very heart of what I believe a theological discussion of music should entail.

Eight days after his birth on the 13th of September, Schoenberg, born of Jewish parents, was circumcised and registered with the Viennese Jewish community, although the extent to which his parents were observant or practising Jews is unclear. His father, Samuel Schönberg, is said to have been a 'free-thinker', a euphemism for an assimilated Jew, while his mother came from a long line of synagogue cantors hailing from Prague.[7] Nevertheless, his baptism into the Lutheran Church at the age of twenty-four and subsequent marriage to his first wife might suggest his own assimilation, but an anti-Semitic incident at the Mattsee hotel in Austria in 1921 precipitated his return to Judaism. Not only did the incident demonstrate to him that Jews could never fully assimilate, particularly now that antisemitism had become racially- rather than religiously-motivated, but it brought home to him a newfound appreciation

---

[6] Cf., for example, R. Castelluci, 'In the Desert', *Arnold: Schoenberg: Moses und Aron (DVD)*, Orchestre et Choeurs de l'Opera National de Paris (2015), p.8.

[7] S. J. Cahn, 'The Viennese-Jewish Experience', in J. Shaw, & J. Auner (eds.), *The Cambridge Companion to Schoenberg* (Cambridge: Cambridge University Press, 2010), p. 193.

of a will to survive on the part of the Jewish people (having endured millennia of prejudice and persecution) which he felt held religious significance and which he considered a religious duty to perpetuate. Thus, in 1922–23 he began to write two works which would pre-empt his final conversion to Judaism in 1933: *The Biblical Way* and *Moses und Aron*.[8]

Moses und Aron is based upon passages taken from the book of Exodus, beginning with God's revelation of Himself to Moses in the burning bush, followed by the journey of the Jewish people through the desert, their idolising of the golden calf, the giving to Moses of the Ten Commandments, and finishes with the departure of the Jewish people for the promised land of milk and honey while the tragic, solitary figure of Moses is left behind. It is Moses' first words, however, which establish the theme for the remainder of the opera and make it a good study case for the discussion of the relationship between music and theology: 'Unique, infinite, omnipresent, unperceived and inconceivable God!' Moses' vocation, as he conceives it, is to introduce this God to His chosen people, the Jews and, as Bluma Goldstein writes, the central focus of the opera is the possibility (or impossibility) of ' ... representing an ineffable deity through language which can only falsify what is essentially unrepresentable'.[9] For Goldstein, however, God's ineffability not only constitutes the plot of the opera but it also informs Schoenberg's own understanding of the Jewish vocation, for which reason the opera focuses solely upon this aspect of the life of faith rather than the numerous other elements of the narrative.[10] But why is this aspect of the story explored to the exclusion of everything else? And why does Schoenberg's libretto open with these words, repeated throughout the opera, which are not present in the original biblical narrative? And why is there a purported difficulty in speaking of God at all? Do we not, after all, have *Torah*, Jesus Christ, *Qu'ran*? Do they not speak of God?

2.1 'Unique, Infinite, Omnipresent, Unperceived and Inconceivable God!'

The problematic has its basis in Abrahamic monotheism's doctrine of Creation. If God is the creator of the universe, as Judaism, Christianity, and Islam hold Him to be, He cannot be a being or object within that universe, because that would mean that some element of the universe, of which God would have to be a part, would already have existed and the question of who created *that* (who,

---

[8] B. Goldstein, *Reinscribing Moses* (Cambridge, MA: Harvard University Press, 1992), pp. 137–141; J. Brown, *Schoenberg and Redemption* (Cambridge: Cambridge University Press, 2014), p. 42; R. Kurth, 'Immanence and Transcendence in *Moses und Aron, Cambridge Companion to Schoenberg*, p. 179.

[9] Goldstein, p. 152.   [10] Ibid., p. 142.

then, created God?) would require an answer. And if the creator of God is a further being within the universe, the question of who created God's creator must then be answered, and so we would be faced with a regress. To put things more bluntly, if we speak of God as though He is a being within the universe we effectively argue that He could not have created it.

For God to have created the universe, then, He would have to occupy a different level of being (or ontological order) *from* the universe, a type of being who is, unlike everything else within the universe, the source of itself ('unoriginate', or uncreated; the necessary existent), the source of all existence and not a result of existence. He must necessarily be of an ontological order to which the language of createdness (which uses terms like 'existence', 'being', the very language I am currently using, in fact) cannot adequately apply. This means that the language of time and space, which belongs to and within the created universe, cannot apply to God because the creator of time and space cannot be subject to time and space. If He were, they would have to have existed before Him which means that He could not have created them. So while we can argue on the one hand that we can say much about God's revelation of Himself in the Torah, Qu'ran, or through His incarnation in Christ, we must recognise the difficulty of discussing what God is like in Himself if we are to respect His (to us, quite unfathomable) ontological status.

A danger to which all discussion of God is repeatedly susceptible, then, is that of *anthropomorphism*, of speaking of Him as though He were but one object among others in the universe. This is how the question 'Who made God?' can be addressed. *If* we believe the faith statement that God is the creator of the universe, then we are bound to accept that this language of createdness cannot be applied to Him, and that the question 'Who made God?' results from a philosophical and categorical error, an anthropomorphism which fails to recognise the God of Abrahamic monotheism.

The question, therefore, is what sort of language *can* be used about the nature and being of God and one answer to this can be found in the development of the *via negativa*, describing God by negative statements only (i.e., by stating what God is *not*, rather than by what He is) or the (closely related) apophatic tradition, which is language about God which acknowledges its own failure to refer to God adequately. Language about God, when it is used at all, is therefore necessarily analogical or metaphorical, language performing *differently*, and can never be taken as literal lest we disrespect His ontological status. As David Burrell writes, 'The aim [...] is to secure the distinction of God from the world, and to do so in such a way as to display how such a One, who must be unknowable, may also be known'.[11]

---

[11] D. B. Burrell, *Knowing the Unknowable God: Ibn-Sina, Maimonides, Aquinas* (Indiana: University of Notre Dame Press, 1986), p. 3.

2.2 Music and the Problem of Representation – Arthur Schopenhauer

The suggestion that Schoenberg fully subscribed to the idea of a God uncontainable by language addressed in *Moses und Aron* is pre-echoed by his fixation with the Second Commandment (which prohibits making images of God and is essentially concerned with idolatry). In the second of his *Four Pieces for Mixed Chorus*, composed in 1925, the text, written by Schoenberg, reads:

> Thou shalt make no image!
> For an image restricts,
> Limits, grasps,
> What should remain unlimited and inconceivable.
>
> An image wants a name:
> You can only take it from below;
> Thou shall not revere the lower!
>
> Thou must believe in the spirit!
> Without mediation, without emotion
> And without self.
> Thou must, chosen one, must, if you want to remain that!

As Bluma Goldstein writes, 'The confluence of an ineffable and spiritual divinity and the obligation of those chosen to comprehend and live with that divinity informs Schoenberg's conception of Moses and Mosaic tradition, Judaism, and the moral obligation of Jews, whether expressed in song, drama, opera, or political programme'.[12]

There is, however, a further influence which pertains more explicitly to music and Schoenberg's understanding of its purpose, and that is the work of the German philosopher, Arthur Schopenhauer (1788–1860). In his major two-volume work, *The World as Will and Representation*, Schopenhauer argued that the world as we perceive it is an illusion, a false *representation* of the real; objects of experience are perceived by us through the prism of time and space and the faculties we employ in order to perceive are also inescapably confined by time and space. Because an object occupies a particular spatial location at a particular moment in time, and because I am similarly bound by time and space, I can only perceive the object from a particular, and necessarily incomplete, perspective. In this respect, then, my perception of the object is, at best, extremely biased and, at worst, complete illusion. But Schopenhauer follows Immanuel Kant in believing that the object must exist in itself (*an sich*) independently of the vagaries of time and space. The worldly perspective,

---

[12] Goldstein, p. 142.

which is all that is available to us, is called the phenomenal realm while the true, objective view of things is called the noumenal realm, and this noumenal realm is not available to we who are inescapably bound by time and space. The phenomenal realm is a temporal and spatial representation of the noumenal realm and, because objective reality must exist beyond time and space (both of which are necessarily perspectival) humanity's perception of the world can only ever be illusory or, at least, very incomplete.[13] But Schopenhauer goes beyond Kant in pursuing the logical conclusion that if the noumenal is unconditioned by time and space it must be *one*, singular and undifferentiated;[14] plurality depends upon *space* and if there is no space there can be no plurality. So while the physical universe or phenomenal realm is a *representation* of the thing-in-itself, the thing-in-itself must be singular. This further step renders the phenomenal realm yet more illusory.

Schopenhauer also differs from Kant by arguing that the one object of which we can have true knowledge is our very selves. This means that, if the world as it is in itself is *one*,

> *We ourselves are the thing in itself.* Consequently, a way *from within* stands open to us to that real inner nature of things to which we cannot penetrate *from without* [. . .] Precisely as such, the *thing-in-itself* can come into consciousness only quite directly, namely *by it itself being conscious of itself.*[15]

However, because my body and intellect are *representations* of the noumenal, attempts to explain the thing-in-itself must necessarily fail because they argue from phenomenal premises. Schopenhauer calls the singular, universal thing-in-itself the

---

[13] Another major influence here, to whom I shall return later, is Plato. In his 'Theory of Art', Plato writes: 'If you look at a bed, or anything else, sideways or endways or from some other angle, does it make any difference to the bed? Isn't it merely that it *looks* different, without *being* different? And similarly with other things [. . .] When the painter makes his representation, does he do so by reference to the object as it actually is or to its superficial appearance? [. . .] The art of representation is therefore a long way removed from truth, and it is able to reproduce everything because it has little grasp of anything, and that little is of a mere phenomenal appearance.' Plato, *The Republic*, tr. D. Lee (London: Penguin Classics, 2007), 589a–589b. In regard to the illusory nature of the phenomenal, it is also worth noting that Eastern philosophy, particularly that of the Hindu *Upanishads* (philosophical texts in Sanskrit), and its dialogue with Platonism form a significant part of Schopenhauer's thought. However, with regard to the *Upanishads*, Bryan Magee writes, the relationship was not one of influence: 'What happened is that, working entirely within the central tradition of Western philosophy [. . .] he arrived at positions which *he then almost immediately discovered* were similar to some of the doctrines central to Hinduism and Buddhism.' B. Magee, *The Philosophy of Schopenhauer* (Oxford: Oxford University Press, 1983), p.15, emphasis original. Magee therefore holds that the relationship was one of confirmation rather than of influence.

[14] The parallels between Schopenhauer's philosophy and the implications of monotheistic belief should not be overlooked.

[15] A. Schopenhauer, *The World as Will and Representation vol.2*, tr. E.F.J. Payne (New York: Dover, 1969), p. 195, emphases original.

Will, our inaccessibility to which is illustrated by describing the relationship between the human intellect and the human will.[16] I am aware of my willing the movements of the object which is my body, and am therefore conscious of the activating power within myself which is my will. However, the intellect operates merely at the surface-level of our will which we cannot control for it controls us;[17] while our intellect acts according to our desires, we cannot choose our desires, which are seated in the will. Thus, while I do as I *will*, I am not free to will otherwise.[18] This is a further distinction between Schopenhauer and Kant and serves as an analogy for the operation of the world as a phenomenal manifestation of the universal Will. The world and everything in it, including my individual will, is a phenomenal representation of the noumenal Will, of which we cannot have direct knowledge. Thus, Schopenhauer writes that '[. . .] the master is the will, the servant the intellect, for in the last instance the will is always in command, and therefore constitutes the real core, the being-in-itself of man'.[19]

For our current purposes, the most important thing to take from Schopenhauer is that when music speaks to the human will it communicates with us at a level deeper than we can comprehend, namely, *at the affective level*. And although the operations of the human will offer a glimpse into the workings of the universal Will, even the human will is beyond our understanding. Therefore, while Schopenhauer might appear to claim knowledge of the thing-in-itself on the basis of its phenomenal representation, we must remain agnostic as to what can be said about the Will.

His theory of aesthetic transcendence consists in escaping the world and attaining to reality as it truly is through contemplation of beauty. This leads to his comparing each of the arts with aspects of the phenomenal realm so, for example, inanimate nature is compared with architecture, organic nature with painting, animality with sculpture, and human intellectuality with poetry and drama. Music, as the least comprehensible and most uncontainable of the arts (because it is imageless and defies semantic description) cannot be paired with anything in the phenomenal realm and is considered a representation of the Will itself. And because what music represents cannot be apprehended by the intellect in linguistic or conceptual terms it communicates more directly to the human person by speaking to his or her will. In other words, *music reaches into the self in a way that the intellect cannot and thereby allows it to transcend itself.*

---

[16] I distinguish between the individual will and the universal 'Will' by use of the lower- and upper-case letters respectively.

[17] Schopenhauer might be considered to have anticipated Freud in this respect.

[18] A. Schopenhauer, *Prize Essay on the Freedom of the Will*, tr. E. F. J. Payne (Cambridge: Cambridge University Press, 1999), pp. 19–21.

[19] Schopenhauer, *WWR2*, p. 208.

It is important to take this a step further by looking at how Schopenhauer believes music makes its emotional impact:

> We must never forget when referring to all these analogies I have brought forward, that music has no direct relation to them, but only an indirect one; for it never expresses the phenomenon, but only the inner nature, the in-itself, of every phenomenon, the [W]ill itself. Therefore music does not express this or that particular and definite pleasure, this or that affliction, pain, sorrow, horror, gaiety, merriment, or peace of mind, but joy, pain, sorrow, horror, gaiety, merriment, peace of mind *themselves*, to a certain extent in the abstract, their essential nature, without any accessories, and so also the motives for them.[20]

In other words, whereas emotions are triggered by phenomenal events (what affect theorists describe as 'occurrent emotions'),[21] music stimulates emotions as they would be in themselves *independent of phenomenal experience*.[22] In this way the contemplation of music allows us to transcend ourselves in the sense that I escape phenomena and attain to my noumenal self. And the difference between emotion as experienced and emotion as it is *an sich* is reflected in that between music, which expresses only itself, and drama, which communicates phenomena:

> If man reflects, he cannot assert any likeness between a piece of music and the things that pass through his mind. For music differs from all the other arts by the fact that it is not a copy of the phenomenon [. . .] but is directly a copy of the [W]ill itself, and therefore expresses the metaphysical to everything physical in the world, the thing-in-itself to every phenomenon.[23]

Thus, with regard to opera, music communicates emotional content which drama merely elucidates – music speaks directly to our affectivity while drama must first traverse the intellect. For this reason, Schopenhauer rejects music which attempts to mould itself to the meaning of the text, for 'endeavouring to speak a language not its own'.[24]

The relevance of Schopenhauer for a discussion of *Moses und Aron* is that he articulated in a clear and (for nineteenth- and early twentieth-century composers,

---

[20] Schopenhauer, *WWR1*, p. 261, emphasis original.
[21] S. Davies, 'Emotions Expressed and Aroused by Music', ed. Sloboda & Juslin, pp. 19–20, 23–24, 33, cf. F. Cova, J. Deonna, & D. Sander, '"That's Deep!" The Role of Being Moved and Feelings of Profundity in the Appreciation of Serious Narratives', in D. R. Wehrs, & T. Blake (eds.), *The Palgrave Handbook of Affect Studies and Textual Criticism* (Cham: Palgrave MacMillan, 2017), pp. 357, 361.
[22] Schopenhauer, *WWR1*, p. 261, cf. *WWR2*, p. 451.   [23] Schopenhauer, *WWR1*, p. 262.
[24] Ibid., p. 262. The influence of this comment can be detected in Schoenberg's comment that 'The assumption that a piece of music must summon up images of one sort of another [. . .] is as widespread as only the false and banal can be'. A. Schoenberg, *Style & Idea: Selected Writings of Arnold Schoenberg*, tr. L. Black (London: Faber & Faber, 1975), p. 141.

including Schoenberg) influential manner that music speaks to the human more deeply than any other medium, that it transcends language and cannot be captured by it.[25] Furthermore, resemblances between Schopenhauer's description of the Kantian noumenal and some of the language I have been using with regard to the divine (transcending time and space, resistant to intellectual containment, etc.) might also be detected. Nevertheless, this is where the analogy between music and the divine seems strongest, in music's ability to signal mystery. And given widespread support for the argument that Schoenberg's primary intention in his opera was to emphasise the difficulty of expressing the inexpressible, his using a musical vehicle seems the most perfect marriage of message with medium.

2.3 Representing the Unrepresentable

In the opera, then, the character of Moses, for whom the medium of speech does not come naturally, employs *sprechtstimme*, a form of unpitched lyrical speech (associated with Schoenberg and employed by him in other works). His brother, Aaron, a charismatic orator, is appointed Moses' spokesman. Aaron sings with a full lyrical tenor voice and is confident that he can give the Hebrews an image of God in which they can believe. However, the two very quickly find themselves at loggerheads over the message they wish to communicate to their followers. Aaron's desire for peoplehood and community is quickly seduced by the need for imagery: 'Can you worship what you dare not even represent?' But their disagreement over the content of the message is symptomatic of their competing conceptions of chosenness. Aaron sees it is privilege and believes that Moses asks too much of God's chosen people, whereas Moses' desire is to free the Hebrews from what is material and transitory: 'Purify your thinking! Free it from what is worthless, dedicate it to what is true: no other reward is given for your sacrifice.'

---

[25] Various commentators agree that Schoenberg followed the ideas of Schopenhauer and Kant, cf. Carl Dahlhaus: 'In 1912 [. . .] Schoenberg was convinced that it was music that expressed the "innermost essence of the world," in the sense of Schopenhauer's metaphysical world view as transmitted through Wagner. It depicted the interior, whereas a text – in vocal music as well as in programme music – depicted merely an exterior.' *Schoenberg and the New Music*, tr. D. Puffett, & A. Clayton (Cambridge: Cambridge University Press, 1987), pp. 166–167; Julie Brown: '[Schoenberg] invoked the musical idea as a type of Kantian transcendental category in the manuscripts of the 1930s, yet had earlier connected it with more expressive impulses [. . . In *Moses und Aron*] Schoenberg brings the "idea into connection with the divine idea, or Word, creating an allegory resonant with the model of Divine Creation."' Brown, p. 179; Richard Kurth: 'No opera articulates the quest for the noumenal more explicitly than Schoenberg's *Moses und Aron*.' p. 177 cf. p. 183; J. Johnson, 'Schoenberg, Modernism, and Metaphysics', *Cambridge Companion to Schoenberg*, pp. 112 & 117; J. Johnson, *Out of Time* (Oxford: Oxford University Press, 2015), p. 172.

But the Hebrews desire to *physicalise* God, to make of Him something material. They reject a God they cannot see and who gives nothing tangible in return for belief. Indeed, they would rather remain in captivity than believe in a God who makes such demands of their faith. But for Moses the desire for the material *is* captivity; as long as the Hebrews demand this kind of God they are not free. And when Moses ascends Mount Sinai to await the revelation of the Law, the people become impatient and demand a return to pagan gods which results in a deity who is in every respect the opposite of that upheld by Moses; they create an idol, a god who can be seen and who satisfies their criteria of beauty and prosperity.

This introduces the golden calf which, being a physical object, can never attain to the heights of the divine. Moreover, the image which they have forged for themselves to worship is *created in their own image*; it reflects the desires they have projected onto it.[26] Whereas in Moses' conception the Hebrews were God's chosen people, they have found self-definition in worshipping a God whom *they* have chosen. By praising this image of power, they give themselves power, for in reality they worship only themselves. The dissenting voice who recognises that submission cannot be genuine if we choose that to which we submit is quickly silenced. Furthermore, by projecting their values and aspirations onto the golden calf they thereby sacralise them and render them physical, and the physicality of the calf justifies their claim that the spirit is sensual: 'Sense first gives to spirit sense.' The sensual is therefore elevated and divinised: 'Those gods who have given you sense and spirit to affect you, let them be exalted!' All order consequently dissolves into chaotic, orgiastic, desire.

When Moses descends from the mountain bearing the Law he laments the Hebrews' bid for freedom by making their god a captive and a slave to the image, proclaiming the superiority of God's words over their image: 'Your image folded at my word.' The image can only be transient for Moses, whereas the word of God is set to endure for ever. For Aaron, however, it is Israel who will endure; he prioritises the people because they are God's chosen people. Moses realises that even the words of the commandments cannot fully express his idea of the divine, whereas Aaron reiterates that the people need something tangible, that the idea must be translated into that which the people can *perceive*. If the words/commands which translate God are also images (because they can be perceived), then the words, too, must be destroyed. Moses therefore smashes the stone tablets containing the commandments rather than risk diminishing the idea of God in any way. Aaron argues that word and image must necessarily emerge from the idea of God if Israel is to be sustained, if their existence is to be

---

[26] Tellingly, before revealing the calf, Aaron cries, 'Revere yourselves in this gold symbol'.

taken as proof of the living God: 'This is my mission: to speak it more simply than I understand it.' The Hebrews then make their way towards Israel, the promised land of milk and honey while Moses, realising that his attempts to express the inexpressible have also resulted in an image, is left in solitude contemplating his failure: 'O word, thou word that I lack!'

Moses und Aron thus raises the problem of how we should understand a God who is uncontainable and inconceivable, indescribable by language but who nevertheless desires relationship with humanity. Rejecting any form of conceptualisation, Moses insists on faith in a God who does not communicate Himself whereas Aaron sees a need for an image. But there is a sense in which in the created world (itself an image) there can only *be* images – the divine can communicate with the creature only through the mediation of the Creation. *Pace* David Burrell, the sensory has to become a means of 'knowing the unknowable God', and Moses has become checkmated by a purported exclusivity between word and image. The question, then, is whether or not there is a correct way of escaping this problem, and the dichotomy Schoenberg presents can be solved only by recognising that idolatry consists not in worshipping an image but in failing to recognise that every image points to its creator.

If, as Judaism, Christianity, and Islam argue, the Creation is divinely ordained, its images cannot in themselves be inherently evil, but what Aaron offered were *false* images of human projection and self-deification, which is pride. Bluma Goldstein argues that, for Schoenberg's Moses, 'the second commandment, which prohibits images of God, is not merely a fundamental condition of Jewish monotheism and a meaningful life, it is virtually the only condition'.[27] I would instead argue that God's irreducibility is something which must first be accepted before anything else can have meaning, that God must not be seen to be an object in the universe over which humanity can take possession. Indeed, recognising God's uncontainability might, in fact, be a *freeing* realisation if it encourages us to look for signs of Him in His creation.

The extent to which Schoenberg recognises this and intended his opera to communicate it is unclear among his commentators. Goldstein writes, 'The ambiguity of this text, in which it is not clear why Moses is to remove his shoes, calls into question the absolute separation of the sacred from the worldly and allows for the possibility that holiness as a way of thinking and being may not be opposed to commonplace living, but an integral part of it'.[28] Indeed, the purported separation between the sacred and the worldly (what is known as the 'Axial' understanding of heaven and earth) is an issue central to the discussion of theology and music to which I shall return in the

---

[27] Goldstein, p. 163.   [28] Ibid., p. 154.

next section but, at this point, it is pertinent to reintroduce Schopenhauer to the discussion in order to examine the influence of his theories upon Schoenberg's *Moses und Aron*.

In *Immanence and Transcendence in Moses und Aron*, Richard Kurth writes that 'The opera is fundamentally concerned with the limits of perception and knowledge, and with the potential for human spirit to supersede those limits', and continues that 'The music's fabric of sound, more than the events portrayed or the ideas articulated by the words, conveys the experience and import of those epistemological limits [...] No opera articulates the quest for the noumenal more explicitly than Schoenberg's *Moses und Aron*'.[29] All of this sounds manifestly Schopenhauerian, not least the claim that it is the music more than anything else which communicates the psychologically unsettling elements of the drama. But Kurth observes the criticisms of Theodor Adorno and Gary Tomlinson that, by trying to represent metaphysics through music, Schoenberg 'loses the possibility of representing the impossibility of representing metaphysics – the most basic premise on which the whole endeavour of *Moses und Aron* was predicated'.[30] Kurth defends Schoenberg of this charge by arguing that *Moses und Aron* 'is a sacred work only in being an extended demonstration of the *impossibility* of conveying the sacred',[31] but I would qualify Kurth's defence on two counts. First, it is not a sacred work '*only*' in being a demonstration of the impossibility of conveying the sacred but precisely *because* it demonstrates this – it underscores the necessity and submissive nature of a faith which will be required to accept and live with mystery. Indeed, for this very reason I would go further and say that it is of the greatest urgency to communicate the idea of unrepresentability itself. Second, I will begin to argue that it is not *impossible* to convey the sacred, it is only impossible to reduce it to what can be contained by us (a realisation which itself constitutes the beginnings of conveying the divine). It is the presumption to contain which constitutes idolatry but this does not necessitate the impossibility of connection at which Schoenberg's Moses seems to arrive. This is why I would reject Kurth's (or Schoenberg's) repeated use of the term 'incomprehensibility' with regard to God and replace it with irreducibility or uncontainability.[32]

But Kurth seems to be veering away from a Schopenhauerian understanding of *Moses und Aron* by claiming that Schoenberg's intention is not to represent

---

[29] R. Kurth, 'Immanence and Transcendence in *Moses und Aron*', in J. Shaw, & J. Auner (eds.), *The Cambridge Companion to Arnold Schoenberg* (Cambridge: Cambridge University Press, 2010), p. 177.

[30] Kurth, p. 177. It would be fair to note that Schopenhauer is also guilty of attempting to represent the unrepresentable, of saying too much about a Will which is purported to be inaccessible.

[31] Kurth, p. 180.   [32] Ibid., pp. 184–185, 188, 190.

the noumenal (given that this is, in fact, impossible) but to take human perception to the very threshold of its phenomenal limits. A comment from a letter Schoenberg wrote to Wassily Kandinsky is telling:

> We must become conscious that there are puzzles around us. And we must find the courage to look these puzzles in the eye without timidly asking about 'the solution'. [. . .] But if we can only learn from them to consider the incomprehensible [*das Unfassbare*] as possible, we get nearer to God, because we no longer demand to understand him. Because then we no longer measure him without intelligence, criticise him, deny him, because we cannot reduce him to that human inadequacy which is our clarity.[33]

Kurth therefore argues that Schoenberg expresses ineffability not through images but through extremely complex musical puzzles (melodic palindromes, combined tetrachords, etc.) contained within the score.[34] And their purpose is to sustain the listeners' critical faculties at the very edge of what is comprehensible in order to point beyond that threshold. In this respect, then, Kurth is subtly turning away from a Schopenhauerian understanding and is instead presenting something which stops just short of that.

Carl Dahlhaus seems to support this claim, albeit for different reasons. Writing that, in 1912, Schoenberg's conception of music certainly did align with Schopenhauerian principles in that music expressed the primordial essence of the universe, and that it portrayed what is interior rather than what is exterior (which is the realm of the text or the programme note), he then continues to claim that

> The relationship between music and language that forms the basis of the dramaturgy of Moses und Aron, coupled with Schoenberg's return to the Jewish faith, one of whose characteristics is to take language emphatically at its word, caused the Schopenhauerian aesthetic, which was accepted unquestioningly by those German composers who preserved the Wagnerian tradition around 1900, to become suspect.[35]

---

[33] J. Hahl-Koch (ed.), *Arnold Schoenberg/Wassily Kandinsky: Letters, Pictures and Documents*, tr. J. C. Crawford (London: Faber, 1984), pp.54–55, quoted in Kurth, pp.183–184.

[34] 'The music of *Moses und Aron* enacts in aural experience these limits of non-verbal thinking and perception [. . .] Schoenberg's music does not communicate [content . . .]; but as a labyrinth or puzzle, the musical artwork does *enact the experience* of such a thought, as a blend of clarity, irreducibility, and incomprehensibility.' Kurth, p. 186.

[35] Dahlhaus continues, 'The programmatic elements in instrumental works, but above all the dominance of vocal music and the character of texts, which are invariably burdened with philosophy or biography and whose verbal form may sometimes be questionable (though their confessional seriousness places them above criticism), force us to come to an interpretation other than the one suggested by Schopenhauer's metaphysical world view, a world view which was created as a philosophy of absolute music and in which texts, programmes and scenic events appear as interchangeable surface phenomena for the music – which alone can penetrate to the profundity of the world. In Schoenberg's late works, the significance of the content has grown in

Whether Dahlhaus is right to characterise the Jewish faith in this way is a discussion for another time, but it is significant that he should cite Schoenberg's embracing of Judaism as a reason for turning away from Schopenhauer when another possibility might be more plausible, namely that Schoenberg conflates the Schopenhauerian 'Idea' and metaphysics with his concept of God *as a result* of his deeper engagement with Judaism, and that the intertwining of his Schopenhauer-influenced musical metaphysics and his concept of God become essential to addressing the inconceivability of God in *Moses und Aron*. As I noted earlier, there are clear resemblances between the language used by Schopenhauer to describe the Will and that used by theology with regard to the divine (i.e., that both transcend time and space and defy intellectual containment, etc.), as well as music's analogical ability to signal divine mystery. This might suggest that some elements of Schopenhauerian philosophy can be thematised more 'religiously' than Schopenhauer himself would have liked, while others can be dispensed with. For example, followers of Abrahamic monotheism must remain circumspect about Schopenhauer not necessarily because of his avowed atheism but because his doctrine of the Will reduces God's creation – the creation which God has endorsed as 'good' (Genesis 1:4, 11, 13, 19, 22, 25, 31) which he cherishes (Surah 1:2), to which He has revealed Himself through the Qu'ran, the Torah, and into which He has entered in the person of Christ – to mere illusion.

However, the monotheist can appreciate and endorse music's capacity for wordless communicability without adopting either the creation–rejecting route of Schopenhauer *or* Kurth's suggestion that Schoenberg used musical puzzles in order to keep the listener at the very edge of what he or she could comprehend. This is because music has enough of its own mystery not to need the type of puzzles that Kurth describes, and even though he can proffer evidence for their existence in the score, I believe we can trust in music's inherent capacity to instantiate mystery (and I very much suspect that Schoenberg wrote *Moses und Aron* because he trusted in it too). And this is because music is *not* a representation of the unrepresentable but an *analogy* for it. As demonstrated by the *Wozzeck* experiment with which I opened my introduction, when confronted with (especially wordless) music, we are faced with something that cannot effectively be described in terms borrowed from another medium. The music simply does what it does and each of us perceives it differently because of what we bring to it. Sometimes one feels that one can describe its effects in words,

---

proportion to the degree that the distinction between the musical means has become irrelevant. It seems that Schoenberg, in the last decades of his life, moved away from absolute music which later became exclusively predominant in the serialism of the 1950s'. Dahlhaus, *Schoenberg and the New Music*, p. 167.

sometimes not, but if one does so one speaks for oneself alone. Music does not *describe* the divine because the divine cannot be described, but if music can take us towards a deeper appreciation of the fact that there are things in life which defy conceptual discussion, but which are nevertheless *meaningful*, it is vital to religion and might be the very thing that makes music sacred, regardless of the tradition in which it is being employed.

2.4 The Philosophical Legitimacy of the Non-Conceptual

> They said, 'You have a blue guitar,
> You do not play things as they are.'
> The man replied, 'Things as they are
> Are changed upon the blue guitar.' (Wallace Stevens)

In order to provide further support for this last point, I shall turn to *Music, Philosophy, and Modernity*, by philosopher Andrew Bowie, in which he addresses our understanding of music by suggesting, *in nuce*, that its capacity to express meaning in a manner which defies conceptual discourse is something from which philosophy and theology might learn. As I have already argued, Abrahamic monotheism requires us to acknowledge mystery in our discussion of God, that it would be a mistake to attempt to reduce God to what can be said. Analogously, Bowie argues that philosophical theories of music risk doing the same, that music's meaning might lie 'precisely in the fact that we cannot say in words what it means'.[36] Put differently, what if music's resistance to conceptual clarification is its very strength and what if our inability to reduce music to what can be said about it is in fact good for us?

Bowie further argues that music is '[a way] of revealing new aspects of being, rather than just a means of re-presenting what is supposedly there'.[37] In other words, music does not merely describe the world as it is but reveals it to us in new ways, allows us to see it differently, and thereby becomes an interpretative category. Music therefore achieves something important which cannot be contained by the conceptual. But Bowie also extends this power to language, noting that 'metaphorical usage causes difficulties for semantic theories which assume the words have specifiable "senses"'.[38] And this is precisely because of the impossibility of context-free interpretation, that the way something is said, where, when, and by whom has considerable bearing upon its purported meaning. Moreover, the affective spaces we inhabit are contingent upon circumstances ranging from the political to the educational and familial. In other words,

---

[36] A. Bowie, *Music, Philosophy, and Modernity, Modernity* (Cambridge: Cambridge University Press, 2007), p. 3.

[37] Ibid., p. 4.   [38] Ibid., p. 4.

our interpretive processes are shaped by factors beyond our control. But while we are educated into ways of perceiving the world, shared by others, we can never arrive at an objective interpretation of it.[39] Thus, language cannot be held to be as prescriptive as some might assume. But because interpretation takes place within a community, it can neither be merely nor purely individualistic.

The corollary of this claim might be that an attempted theology of music is a mistake if music defies discussion,[40] but the point is that if music can reveal to us the limits of the conceptual by transcending them, this might be precisely what a theology of music should be; theology which emerges out of its inability to contain music. Music might thus become an instructive ally for, as has already been established, the monotheistic Abrahamic faiths require us to believe in more than what can be objectified and the experience of music (or aesthetic experience more generally) demonstrates that we often do this in other areas of our lives. Indeed, as Bowie writes, 'If cognitive content is supposed to be exclusively propositional, too many non-propositional states will be excluded which can tell us much about ourselves and the world'.[41] Bowie thus upholds our reaction to music as a means of demonstrating the weaknesses of verificationism but he also denies the claim that it expresses emotions with which we are already familiar, such as sadness and happiness,[42] because this suggests that music is merely describing things already known to us rather than revealing aspects of the world which would otherwise remain undisclosed. Thus, when Schopenhauer writes that 'music does not express this or that particular and definite pleasure, this or that affliction, pain, sorrow, horror, gaiety, merriment, or peace of mind, but joy, pain, sorrow, horror, gaiety, merriment, peace of mind *themselves*, to a certain extent in the abstract, their essential nature, without any accessories, and so also the motives for them',[43] he is recognising that *music introduces into the world things which are not already there*. Theology can therefore learn much from Schopenhauer even if we reject some of his most central metaphysical presuppositions.

Music, then, like faith, conditions our relationship to God and the world and *vice versa* (i.e., faith shapes our relationship with music), and the dialectical relationship between the two means that if each affects how the other is

---

[39] Ibid., pp. 9–10.   [40] Ibid., p. 11.

[41] Ibid., p. 20. cf. C. Marsh, V. S. Roberts, 'In contrast to a worldview approach that would too easily place emphasis on *cognitive* elements of human formation [. . .] ideas and beliefs are but part of many aspects of what it means to be human. It is *desire* that drives us, and therefore our emotions, our guts, and our heart are primarily what steer us'. C. Marsh, & V. S. Roberts, *Personal Jesus: How Popular Music Shapes Our Souls* (Grand Rapids, MI: Baker Academic, 2012), p. 35.

[42] P. Kivy, *Introduction to a Philosophy of Music* (Oxford: Clarendon Press, 2002), p. 31, quoted in Bowie, p. 21.

[43] Schopenhauer, WWR1, p. 261, emphasis original.

interpreted, each provides the context for the other. To this we can add language, which may appear surprising given its associations with the conceptual, but if we accept that the manner and context in which something is said dramatically affects how it functions it can assume world-disclosive, as well as descriptive, capacities. Furthermore, as science comes to form the bedrock of objectivity and certainty, as has increasingly become the case throughout the Modern period, appreciation for that realm of life which resists measurement and objectification and which is dealt with by music and poetry (and, I would add, faith) grows in direct proportion; in the void left by the scientistic, materialist approach to human experience, faith and music come into play. And if the scientistic approach arises from a need to be in *control* of nature there is an element of freedom from certainty (the importance of which has already been emphasised) in the more 'aesthetic' approach which is liberating.

What is being argued, then, is that there is an affective level of understanding which does not require conceptual translation if one accepts the possibility of a non-cognitive relationship to the world. Bowie's proposals need not suggest a religious realm,[44] but it should now be clear that music can assist monotheistic theology which is resistant to descriptive language regarding the divine by emphasising the possibility of a non-cognitive relationship with God. This also informs our approach to Scriptural interpretation and exegesis: without an affective appreciation for the context in which the text is 'carried out', it becomes reduced to the semantic level and its truth is lessened. If this is accepted it suggests that by aiming for understanding purely on the conceptual level one risks apprehending less truth; if clarity can only be achieved conceptually, then what we can achieve clarity *about* is limited and other, possibly more important, dimensions of existence risk being neglected.

One of the dangers which might arise, of course, and which I shall later address more fully, is that if music is to be seen as mystery in its own right it might be held to be in competition with the mystery of God. But what I am arguing here is that music is necessary for theology and worship because it provides an immediate, temporal, tangible mystery which defies intellectual interpretative categories, thereby affirming that this realm exists for the human person regardless of religious belief. It thus demonstrates that the positivistic, materialist, or scientistic realm is insufficient for philosophy and that mystery has a legitimate place in philosophical and theological discourse rather than something behind which one retreats when logical answers fail us, as they must inevitably do when engaging in speech about God.

---

[44] It is important to observe that Bowie does not appear to subscribe to a faith position.

If any of this has theological purchase, it suggests that while Schoenberg may have exaggerated or overstated the meaning of the Second Commandment in *Moses und Aron*, he is not wrong to emphasise it. Faith demands submission of the self to the divine, not to things we can see and possess, and the significance of music's 'unsayability' lies in its resistance to intellectual containment. If it is accepted that to understand is to be in control then this chafes against the decentring required by the life of faith. Furthermore, is our faith in the divine purely predicated upon intellectual argument or might there not be aspects of our lives, both inside and outside the synagogue, church, or mosque, perhaps more 'aesthetic', affective, or non-cognitive moments, which contribute significantly to what we believe? What we learn from trying to understand music in the manner being proposed here, then, is that the idol in *Moses und Aron* is not the Golden Calf, neither is it the word in the form of the stone tablets. The idol is intellectual control. The idol is the self.

3 A Great Separation?

> I have lived with the hope that perhaps there are not two realms, the sacred world of God and the profane world of Gentile art, but that great art can also be for the sake of heaven.
>
> Chaim Potok, *The Gift of Asher Lev*

3.1 Music and Islam

Reading Islamic scripture and texts about Islam as a Christian, one cannot help but be struck by its emphasis on monotheism. It is not simply the fact that the first of the Five Pillars is the *shahada*, the testimony of faith that 'There is no god but God', but that it is concentration upon this belief more than anything else which sustains the Muslim in his or her faith.[45] If the way of Islam is the 'straight path' (Sur. 1:6) of monotheism (*tawhīd*), repeated petitions of the *shahada* remind the Muslim that anything which risks becoming a deviation is against Islam. Indeed, the idea of ascribing partners to God, placing anyone or anything else alongside Him, or suggesting that His attributes may be shared by another (*shirk*) is considered the one sin that God will not forgive.[46] But *shirk* does not simply refer to idols such as the Golden Calf of *Moses und Aron* or

---

[45] Celene Ibrahim describes the *shahada* as the gateway into Islam as well as its conceptual heartbeat. C. Ibrahim, *Islam and Monotheism* (Cambridge: Cambridge University Press, 2022), pp. 36–37.

[46] Surah 4:48: 'Allah forgiveth not that partners should be set up with Him: but He forgiveth anything else, to whom He pleaseth; to set up Partners with Allah is to devise a sin most heinous indeed.' Cf. C. Hewer, *Understanding Islam: The First Ten Steps* (London: SCM Press, 2006), pp. 75, 91, 166.

polytheism (which is how Christian Trinitarianism might well appear in the eyes of non-Christians), it can also refer to deviating from the 'straight path' by following one's own whims and desires, by idolising what benefits the self.[47]

Gaining an appreciation of this understanding of and strict adherence to monotheism helps provide some context for a discussion of the place of music within the Islamic faith where, as is the case with Judaism and Christianity, there are differing views and accounts as to what is apposite and what should be excluded.[48] Although I will attempt to give some account of the shape this debate takes within Islam, it is important to go beyond the arguments and show how they might contribute to a wider theology of music which could help inform inter-religious dialogue. It is doubtless the case that some of these arguments have their complements within the other Abrahamic religions so it may well be that each has something positive to learn from the freedoms and strictures of the other.

What appears central to the discussion about music in Islam is how the human person *reacts* to it (indeed, this seems to be more pressing than the nature of the music itself). In other words, for some, the recognition that the human body can react to music with ecstasy is deemed positive, some Sufi writers considering music (and dance, as a physical response to it) as ' . . . a means to spiritual union with the divine (and thus spiritual ecstasy)'.[49] For others, the fact that music can have such somatic power over the human might render it a physical distraction from the upright path of the Muslim and is therefore inimical to the aspirations of Islam.[50] What complicates matters further is the problem that the Qur'an provides nothing authoritative on the issue and guidance is therefore sought from elsewhere, that is, from commentators whose views differ according to the contexts within which music can be heard and their own judgement upon those

---

[47] Cf. Sura 45:23: 'Have you considered one who takes his caprice as his god? And God knowingly let him go astray and sealed his hearing and his heart and placed a cover in his sight. Who then will guide him after God? Will you not then remember?' Cf. Hewer, p. 91.

[48] Leonard Lewisohn writes of 'advocates, adversaries, and moderates'. L. Lewisohn, 'The Sacred Music of Islam: Samā' in the Persian Sufi Tradition', *British Journal of Ethnomusicology*, vol. 6 (1997), pp. 1–33, cf. p. 2. Amnon Shiloah describes the debate as 'interminable' and writes that 'In all the major centres of Islam extending from India, Indonesia and Central Asia to Africa [. . .] all took part in this debate which elicited views that vary from complete negation to full admittance of all musical forms including the controversial dance'. A. Shiloah, 'Music and Religion in Islam', *Acta Musicologica*, July–December, Vol. 69, Fasc. 2 (July–December, 1997), pp. 143–155, cf. p. 143. Published by: International Musicological Society, www.jstpr.org/stable/932653 accessed 2/04/2023.

[49] K. Nelson, *The Art of Reciting the Qur'an* (Austin: University of Texas Press, 1985), p. 32.

[50] Ibid. Lewisohn regards the *pro* and *contra* as 'but a reflection of much wider debates and differences which had existed between Islamic puritanism and mysticism from the earliest days of Islam – the former group stressing divine transcendence and the role of Law and the latter camp emphasising the power of faith, immanence and Love'. Lewisohn, p. 3. This section will address the numerous forms this debate assumes within all three Abrahamic religions, as well as in Classical Greek philosophy.

contexts.[51] In other words, if the texts set to music are inappropriate, if the place in which the music is heard is considered profane (such as a brothel or drinking house), or if the people performing the music are considered irreverent or are inappropriately dressed, the act of listening to it will be discouraged as something which will distract the listener from the life of holiness.[52] So *what* is being sung, *who* is singing it, and *where* the music is being heard are all factors upon which the Muslim is asked to base his or her judgement. But these are not remarks about the music itself, they are judgements upon the things with which the music is associated.

This is an important comment to make upon the discussion of music within theology, because music is often regarded as sacred or otherwise on the basis of its context, the text being sung, the building in which it is heard, the instruments accompanying, and so on, but the question of what makes the music *itself* sacred or otherwise is often dealt with inefficiently. Are there certain notes, harmonies, rhythms which are inherently sacred or non-sacred or are such judgements usually made about music on the basis of other factors which are extrinsic to it? When Shah Abdul Halim writes that 'sensuous music which might incite such prohibited practices as consumption of drugs and alcohol, sex beyond marital bond, etc.',[53] it is reasonable to ask: which are the notes, rhythms, and harmonies which can 'incite' such behaviour and to what extent is their capacity to do so attributable to association and context rather than the actual sounds created? If we accept from the earlier discussion of Andrew Bowie that music itself cannot communicate concepts without the assistance of other media, the question of what makes music itself sacred becomes extremely difficult to answer. It would be entirely correct to argue that music is always experienced within a context of some kind and that the associations it accrues are therefore valid, but this means that if music usually performed in one location (or type of location) can be moved to another its associations must therefore change.[54] Much of the music for Johann Sebastian Bach's *Mass in B Minor* was originally

---

[51] Lois Ibsen al Faruqi, 'Music, Musicians, and Muslim Law', *Asian Music*, Vol. 17, No. 1 (Autumn – Winter, 1985), pp.3–36, University of Texas Press. www.jstor.org/stable/833739 accessed 2/4/2023, pp. 3–4.

[52] For commentary on the conditions under which music can *positively* be performed according to the rules of Sufism ('time, place, and associates'), see Lewisohn, pp.8–15, cf. Ibsen al Faruqi, p. 17.

[53] Shah Abdul Halim, *Music and Islam* (Dhaka: Islamic Information Bureau Bangladesh, 2017), p. 11.

[54] A creative possibility for music's communicability consists in the merging of associations between two quite different types of location so that the listener can be reminded of one place while residing in another. Technological advances mean that the *muezzin* can now be heard in the home. Some might consider this a profanation of the sacred while others might argue that bringing the mosque into the home renders it a more 'sacred' space.

composed for scenarios which were not explicitly sacred (such as royal or state occasions); while the texts for the original occasions were abandoned and replaced with the words of the Eucharist, the music largely remained the same. Similarly, Shah Abdul Halim writes that 'Jalal al-Din Rumi often took songs from the taverns of Anatolia and converted them into vehicles for the expression of the most profound yearning for Allah'.[55] The implication, then, is that if the texts are changed but the music remains the same, it is not the music, but the words, which are problematic. It also means that if music sets a sacred text, it is the words that are sacred for the music could just as easily be used for a different kind of text. For the theologian of music, this is a crucial distinction.

A second angle which emerges from the Islamic discussion of music (or the Samā' polemic, as it is known)[56] is the centrality of ethical behaviour for Muslims which, of course, derives from the understanding of monotheism described earlier.[57] *Tawḥīd* demands that Muslims remain on the 'straight path', and numerous verses in the Qur'an connect focus on the one true God with high ethical standards. When moral virtue is prioritised, it is unsurprising that the aesthetic is considered a poor competitor. As Kristina Nelson observes, '. . . it was felt by many Muslims that music was essentially a frivolous, if not abhorrent, vanity having little to do with the things that matter in this life or the next'.[58] This might be an argument with which many Jews and Christians would also sympathise but, again, this is not an argument against music per se. It is, instead, an argument about what the religious follower *does* with his or her aesthetic reaction, about what place it occupies within his or her journey of faith. As I argued earlier, while a text might be problematic, it is very difficult to identify which aspects of music itself require censure. The following comment from Imam Al-Ghazâlî (c.1056–1111) is somewhat helpful. Reporting that Ibn Jurayj (d.767)

> was wont to allow listening to music and singing and that it was said to him, 'Will this be brought on the day of resurrection among thy good deeds or thy evil deeds?' He said, 'Neither in the good deeds nor the evil deeds, for it is like idle talk, and God Most High has said, "Allah will not call you to account for thoughtlessness in your oaths"'. (Sur. 2:225)[59]

In other words, music is neither moral nor immoral, for these are the wrong categories to apply to it; music would be problematic if it distracts the Muslim

---

[55] Halim, p. 49.

[56] Shiloah notes that Samā' 'designates first and foremost passive listening to music, and only by implication indicates active expression and the making of music'. Shiloah, p. 149.

[57] 'Belief in the oneness of God is not just an intellectual thing, it also requires action.' Hewer, p. 75.

[58] Nelson, p. 38, cf. Halim, p. 13. Nelson later writes, 'The attitude which unequivocally repudiates music is characterised by a puritanical suspicion of everything pleasurable [. . .] It is the view of those who regard all which does not contribute directly to salvation as frivolous'. Nelson, p. 44.

[59] Quoted in Nelson, p. 40.

from the path of virtue (i.e., if he or she over-indulges in it) but, otherwise, its function is not a moral one, and it is therefore harmless. Al-Ghazâlî is therefore being cited here as an ally against the censuring of music in Islam but his praise for it (at least here) seems faint. The comment suggests that, while he considers music harmless, he does not hold it in the highest esteem and certainly does not seem to accord it the vital world-disclosive functions that we found in Bowie. Nor does it seem likely that those who consider music harmless at best would allow the possibility that aesthetic euphoria alone (i.e., a musical/aesthetic experience free of any text) be considered in some way a sacred experience (something I will later ask the reader to consider).

Accounts regarding the views of the Prophet himself are inconsistent. According to some commentators, Mohammed seems not to have liked certain instruments, particularly stringed and reeded instruments (*mazamir*)[60] but is also held to have commented upon beautiful melodic recitations of the Qur'an and is recorded to have enjoyed listening to music with his companions.[61] The most authoritative sources are therefore inconclusive on the matter and thus judgement is predicated upon whether or not a life influenced by music can lead the follower to un-Islamic behaviour or not.

A further argument in favour of music within Islam is the fact that its origins are held to lie in poetry, and the centrality of poetry for the Muslim is another aspect of Islam which is striking to the enquiring Christian. Whereas singing is regarded a mere pastime, poetry, in Islam, is considered the highest art *par excellence* and, since it invites sung recitation, has endowed singing with a prestige it might otherwise have lacked. Poetry was also approved of by the Prophet, and he enjoined its use against non-Muslims.[62] Singing therefore gained some legitimacy by clinging to the coat-tails of poetry but, again, this

---

[60] David Irving notes that there are diverging opinions as to whether Mohammed liked these instruments or not, and that confusion has arisen as to whether he understood the term as referring to a piped instrument or to a voice. D. Irving, 'Psalms, Islam, and Music: Dialogues and Divergence about David in Christian-Muslim Encounters of the Seventeenth Century', *Yale Journal of Music & Religion*, vol. 2, no. 1, article 3 (2016), pp.53–78. https://doi.org/10.17132/2377-231X.1040. Accessed 2/4/2023, pp. 59–60.

[61] Nelson, pp. 42–43. Lewisohn writes, '[. . .] the Koran attests that the purpose of its reminder to humankind is for the Prophet to "make clear to men what has been divinely revealed," and had leaping – which is a form of dancing – belonged to the category of doubtful or harmful or irreligious acts, it would have been necessary for the Prophet to have said so [. . .] dance is the very blossoming of ecstasy and ecstasy is both the cause of dance and the effect of music'. Lewisohn, p. 26. Ibsen al Faruqi writes, 'The religious chants, chanted poetry, family and celebration music, and occupational music, as well as the brass and percussion music of the military bands, have been so consistently supported by incidents from the life of the Prophet Mohammed and his followers, that little time or energy has been spent on countering their acceptance and use'. Ibsen al Faruqi, p. 12.

[62] Nelson, p. 47.

means that music is being judged upon its combination with text, that is, by something extrinsic to it rather than upon its own merits or weaknesses.

However, the fact that melodic recitation of poetry dates from pre-Islamic Arabia might suggest something about the naturally melodic nature of language itself. The eighteenth-century French philosopher Etienne de Condillac argued that language evolved out of musical cries of passion, and that the same cry being melodically inflected depending upon the passion being experienced suggests that language is created *via* musical means; because people imitate each other and meaning is learned, cries become signs. He then argued that signs became standardised and the use of new signs augmented the intellect, thereby improving signification. The key element is that the link between sound and emotion precedes language, that melody existed before linguistic standardisation.[63]

Jean-Jacques Rousseau adopted and developed this theory, ascribing a particularly powerful *emotional* impact to verbal media because cries communicate passions. Vocal sounds, for Rousseau, reach deeper into the self than reading the written word or apprehending the physical gesture because the aural internalises the message and more profoundly connects persons with each other.[64] But Rousseau also argued that vocal signs relate to desire rather than need; for Rousseau, needs create division, but passions join people and are, therefore, a uniquely human concern;[65] whereas animals have needs, only humans have passions, hence the uniqueness of language for human beings.[66] Because language pertains to the passions, then, it is primarily poetic, only later becoming analytical and rational, and thus, for Rousseau, melody retains some connection to its origins, which explains the affective power it commands over its listeners.

Whether or not we accept this theory (which almost certainly developed quite independently of Islam) would be to miss the point that it demonstrates the importance of poetry, of language performing differently, and how it is regarded across different cultures throughout history. It also illustrates the importance of how our apprehension of the linguistic message is *affective* as well as intellectual and may hold some explanatory power when we consider that Qur'anic recitation (like Torah recitation in the synagogue or intoned psalms in certain Christian traditions) is often melodically rendered. Kristina Nelson writes that 'The impulse to render the Qur'anic text melodically has been irresistible from

---

[63] 'At the origin of languages the manner of articulation allowed inflections of voice that were so distinct [. . .] and so I would say that the manner of articulation partook of the quality of chant.' Etienne Condillac, *Essay on the Origin of Human Knowledge*, tr. H. Aarsleff (Cambridge: Cambridge University Press, 2001), p. 121.

[64] Jean-Jacques Rousseau, *Essay on the Origin of Languages*, tr. J. H. Moran (Chicago, IL: Chicago University Press, 1966), p. 8.

[65] Ibid., p. 11.   [66] Rousseau, p. 10.

the beginning of its practice',[67] and records that the power of the recited Qur'an could incite its hearers to 'swooning or even dying'.[68] Indeed, Leonard Lewisohn writes that 'Poetry and words, as vehicles capable of communicating the Transcendental, are themselves highly inadequate. Music alone is capable of bridging the gap between the literal and anagogic levels of meaning'.[69] If the theories of Condillac and Rousseau carry any weight at all, then, it could suggest that melodic recitation speaks to something primordial within the human being because linguistic understanding itself evolved melodically.

However, it is not unambiguously clear that melodic recitation of the Qur'an itself is always approved of, some of the reasons for which resonate with Judaism and Christianity. Al-Ghazâlî held that the Qur'an should not be subjected to musical embellishment due to music's potentially un-Islamic associations but, moreover, because the purity of the Qur'an should not be compromised.[70] Indeed, what is most interesting for our wider discussion here is his insistence that the heavenly Qur'an and the worldly realm be kept separate.[71] This principle of separation between God and world has its complement in both Judaism and Christianity and, again, might be found to have derived from monotheism. But I would like to turn to two different excerpts from Western Classical Music in order to demonstrate the point by way of musical examples.

3.2 Bach, Beethoven, and the Reconciliation of Opposites

In *Beethoven and the Voice of God*, Wilfrid Mellers argues that one finds in Beethoven's work a musical analogue for the Hegelian concept of the *conjunctio oppositorium* (the unity of opposites) which, according to Mellers, finds its fullest expression in the *Missa Solemnis*, where 'The segregation of a God "up there" from Nature "here around" us is [eventually] abolished'. Mellers further argues that '[...] to find God, which is to find the Self, is also to heal the breach between Man and Nature, wherein God *must* be manifest'.[72]

However, if we are properly to discuss Beethoven's representation of the divine in his most substantial sacred work, we must first learn something of his doctrine of God. Birgit Lodes records that

> In 1816, Beethoven noted in his diary: 'God is immaterial, He is above all conception; as He is invisible, He can have no form; but from what we learn

---

[67] Nelson, p. 32.   [68] Ibid., p. 48, cf. Lewisohn, p. 19.   [69] Lewisohn, p. 15.

[70] '[...] the Koran has certain liturgical limitations due to its prearranged system of cantillation which only permit its use in a highly ritualised manner. One is not permitted, for instance, to set its verses to music'. Lewisohn, p. 20.

[71] Nelson, pp. 48–49.

[72] W. Mellers, *Beethoven and the Voice of God* (London: Faber & Faber, 1983), p. 368.

of his works, we may conclude that he is eternal, omnipotent, knowing all things, present everywhere [. . .] For God, time absolutely does not exist.'[73]

This account might not appear especially radical and seems quite in keeping with the understanding of monotheism with which we have been working. However, describing God solely by His negative attributes reintroduces our question not only of how we can relate to Him, but of how He can relate to us. As Hugh Turner observes, 'While this whole framework lends metaphysical stability to the doctrine of God, it emphasises the ontological implications of deity rather than the character and activity of the living God'.[74] There is therefore a serious question about how to conceive the impact of this God upon a humanity which suffers, is subject to change, is contained within time and space and therefore appears to stand in an antithetical relationship to its Creator. This, for some, is Beethoven's concern in the *Missa Solemnis*, that it represents a reaction to God from the human standpoint. But because Beethoven is working with the text of the Ordinary of the Mass and is therefore assumed to be working within a Christian framework it will be important to investigate what presence, if any, the person of Christ has in this work.

In 'The Human and the Divine in the Gloria of Beethoven's Missa Solemnis', Birgit Lodes argues that Beethoven's doctrine of God and his sceptical view of the Church resulted in his taking a fresh and reflective approach to the text of the Mass. She also notes that his theological library included censured books, including Ignaz Aurelius Fessler's *Views about Religion and the Church*, which argues that 'God's spiritual realm exists apart from and above the dogmatic church or other religious institutions', and subsequently argues that

> The structure of Beethoven's Gloria is based on a continual opposition of two textual elements or levels, the 'heavenly/divine' and the 'earthly/human'. Because this opposition is never reconciled, and because the movement ends inconclusively, one can view the Gloria as an expression of Beethoven's perception that man can attempt to achieve at least a conditional understanding of God, but can never fully apprehend Him.[75]

Fessler's argument might not necessarily suggest that God is inaccessible to mankind, of course; it could easily be interpreted as saying that there is a way to God outside of the Church, as a challenge to the institution's claim to be the way, the truth, and the life. This would be in keeping with the dim view of the

---

[73] B. Lodes, 'When I try, now and then, to give musical form to my turbulent feelings: The Human and the Divine in the Gloria of Beethoven's *Missa Solemnis*', *Beethoven Forum 6*, Lincoln, Nebraska University Press (1998), pp. 143–179 (174); Mellers, 1983, p. 292.

[74] H. E. W. Turner, *Jesus the Christ* (London: Mowbray, 1976), p. 30.

[75] Lodes, 1998, pp. 146–147.

Church held by Beethoven himself. Nevertheless, Lodes holds that this movement depicts an irreconcilable gulf between God and humanity, and that Beethoven achieves this by dividing the text into alternating sections representative of this polarity. In order to cement the dichotomy further, Beethoven, according to Lodes, then sets the 'heavenly/divine' sections of the text to one kind of music, and the 'earthly/human' portions to another, arguing that '[. . .] the two musical ideas have virtually nothing in common but their key and time signature', and further holds that 'The sharp contrast between the two sections and their lack of mediation form the basis of the structure of the Gloria and, indeed, for the later movements of the Mass'.[76] This scheme is established at the very beginning of the movement, where Lodes perceives connections between the music accompanying *Gloria in excelsis Deo* and those 'heavenly/divine' sections which are to follow, and likewise for the music which accompanies *et in terra pax hominibus*, representing the 'earthly/human' aspect of the movement.

Because the theological ramifications of this proposal are significant, it is worth investigating whether Beethoven's scheme, as recounted by Lodes, holds up by setting out the purported divisions of the text:

'Heavenly/Divine'	**'Earthly/Human'**
Gloria in excelsis Deo, (Glory to God in the highest)	
	et in terra pax hominibus bonae voluntatis. (and on earth, peace, goodwill, to all men)
Laudamus te, benedicimus te, adoramus te, glorificamus te. (We praise thee, we bless thee, we worship thee, We glorify thee)	
	Gratias agimus tibi propter magnam gloriam tuam. (We give thanks to thee for thy great glory)
Domine Deus, Rex coelestis, (Lord God, heavenly king)	
	Domine fili unigenite (only begotten Son)

---

76 Lodes, 1998, pp. 147–149.

'Heavenly/Divine'	**'Earthly/Human'**
Deus pater omnipotens (O God, almighty Father)	
	Jesu Christe (Jesus Christ)
Domine Deus, agnus Dei, (Lord God, Lamb of God)	
	Qui tollis peccata mundi (Who takest away the sins of the world)
Filius patris. (Son of the Father)	
	miserere nobis, *qui tollis pecata mundi,* *suscipe deprecationem nostrum,* (Have mercy on us, Who takes away the sins of the world, Receive our prayer)
qui sedes ad dexteram patris, (Who sits at the right hand of the Father)	
	Misere nobis (Have mercy on us)
qui sedes ad dexteram patris, (Who sits at the right hand of the Father)	
	miserere nobis (Have mercy on us)
Quoniam tu solus (For you alone	
	sanctus are Holy)
[*quoniam*] *tu solus dominus,* [*quoniam*] *tu solus altissimus,* *Jesu Christe, cum sancto spiritu* *In Gloria Dei patris, amen.* [*Gloria in excelsis Deo, Gloria.*] (For you alone are the Lord You alone are the most high Jesus Christ, with the Holy Spirit, In the glory of God the Father, Amen.)	

While the principle of a musical distinction between *Gloria in excelsis Deo* and *et in terra pax* is common procedure within the Viennese Mass tradition, the strictness with which the segregation between the two textual 'realms' is upheld musically is certainly remarkable and forms the basis of Lodes' argument that the divine and human spheres are never reconciled. However, bars 281–290, *qui sedes ad dexteram Patris, miserere nobis*, do not conform to Lodes' scheme: at this point texts from both realms are being sung simultaneously. The solo quartet sing the words *miserere nobis* (have mercy on us), which, being a plea from humanity to the divine, Lodes categorises as an 'earthly' text, but the choir sing *qui sedes ad dexteram patris* (who sits at the right hand of the Father), which Lodes allots to the 'heavenly' realm. Indeed, it is precisely this short section which Lodes appears to have overlooked which might provide the key to a different interpretation of the *Gloria* for, by conflating these two sections of the text, Beethoven reconciles the 'heavenly' and 'earthly' realms and thereby provides us with a musical working of Romans 8:34, that 'It is Christ Jesus [. . .] who is at the right hand of God, who intercedes for us'.

Indeed, once this reconciliation between the two spheres has taken place, the music remains 'heavenly' until the end of the movement,[77] as if man has been sanctified by the conjoining of the two realms and has been taken up, with or through Christ, into the divine. And while some might object that the music simply reflects the fact that the remainder of the text is 'heavenly', it should be borne in mind that there is nothing to prevent Beethoven's repeating earlier textual moments which would re-separate the two realms. Indeed, the opening line of the text is repeated at the end, so it would not be wrong to attach significance to the fact that, once the reconciliation has taken place in bars 281–90, the remainder of the movement belongs to the 'divine' sphere.

Comparing Beethoven's setting of the *Gloria* with Johann Sebastian Bach's rendering in the *B Minor Mass*, is instructive, and might reveal not only the possible differences in outlook of the two composers, but how these differences might be conveyed musically. For the *Domine Deus* section of the *Gloria* of the *B Minor Mass*, Bach writes an imitative duet for tenor and soprano. Because the words *Domine Deus rex coelestis* (Lord God, heavenly king) are first sung by the tenor, while the words *Domine fili unigenite* (Lord, the only-begotten Son) are sung by the soprano, Wilfrid Mellers argues that the tenor personifies the Father while the Soprano personifies the Son.[78] That the soprano part would originally have been sung by a boy aids this depiction, but a brief analysis of the music quickly demonstrates that Mellers' scheme of personification is entirely

---

[77] Apart from the single bar which sets the word *sanctus*, which means 'holy' or 'set apart'. Beethoven has quite literally set this bar apart from everything around it.

[78] W. Mellers, *Bach and the Dance of God* (London: Faber & Faber, 1980), p. 194.

misleading. Each portion of the text is in fact shared equally between the two soloists, and they alternate between the two lines with strict regularity. In other words, although the tenor does sing *Domine Deus* in the first phrase, while the soprano follows with *Domine fili*, in the second phrase it is the soprano who leads with *Domine Deus* while the tenor follows with *Domine fili*. This pattern of alternation remains for the rest of the movement, until the phrase *Domine Deus, Agnus Dei, Filius Patris* (Lord God, Lamb of God, Son of the Father) which both voices sing together three times.

It is difficult to imagine a more effective way of communicating the Trinitarian belief that the Father and the Son are one,[79] and because Bach alternates the texts between the voices with such systematic regularity, I would submit that this was his intention. However, it is significant that he is able to hold the two together with consummate ease. An examination of the same moment in the text in Beethoven's setting reveals something quite different.

Lodes argues that the closest we come to any mediation between the two realms of God and Man in Beethoven's *Gloria* is in the line *Domine fili unigenite*, which is set to 'earthly music', thereby emphasising the humanity of Christ. According to her scheme, however, we can see that 'after Beethoven greets the incarnate Son with music of the human sphere, he emphasises Christ's divine nature: in the following line, which also addresses Christ (*Domine Deus, agnus Dei*), the *Gloria* [theme] is played by the orchestra'.[80] It is perhaps because the human Christ is so swiftly taken back into the divine sphere that Lodes will allow a mediation, but not a reconciliation between the human and the divine.

Mellers' chapter on the *Gloria* of the *Missa Solemnis* similarly argues that Beethoven seeks to portray a separation between God and Man by the juxtaposition of contrasting sections of music, although his approach is based more upon the orchestration of the movement. For example, he notes that Beethoven first uses the trombones on the word *omnipotens*, and then silences them for 154 bars, thereby reinforcing the 'otherness' of God.[81] He also attributes significance to Beethoven's use of a solo quartet as well as a chorus, arguing that the soloists represent the individual, while the chorus portray humanity as a whole.[82] Unfortunately, the potential of this is never fully or consistently explored, and if there is any theological significance in the way the two groups are used or

---

[79] John McDade posits that the flute obbligato part represents the Holy Spirit; J. McDade, 'The Trinity and the Paschal Mystery', *Heythrop Journal*, vol. xxix (1988), pp. 175–191, p. 176.

[80] Lodes, 1998, p. 152.

[81] Mellers, 1983, p. 307. This is one of dozens of interpretations which might be offered for this musical event, as demonstrated by the *Wozzeck* experiment I described at the opening of this essay.

[82] Ibid., p. 308.

juxtaposed, Mellers does not account for it. Where he differs from Lodes, however, is that for Mellers, '[Beethoven's] God, as compared with man's *pax*, seems a disruptive, even destructive, force',[83] and continues that the movement is 'built on a violent opposition between God's maelstrom and man's attempt at civilised conformity'.[84] The perceived gulf between Man and God is therefore even more extreme in Mellers than in Lodes.

Perhaps ironically, Mellers considers that the juxtaposition between the high tessitura for sopranos, altos and tenors and the basses' descent on the words *qui sedes ad dexteram patris* at bar 270 serves to *separate* Christ from suffering humanity,[85] but this seems another example of subjective interpretation of the music which is in conflict with the evidence presented by the score; Mellers has also missed the conflation of the 'divine' and 'human' texts and therefore does not consider that this moment leads to a union between the human and the divine.

While Lodes and Mellers offer the type of analytical interpretation of music some might prefer to resist (indeed, it is the type of subjective/conceptual interpretation of music I warned against at the outset), they do offer a way of listening to Beethoven's movement which has some value although, as I have shown, an opposing interpretation can be offered. To analyse and interpret the movement from Bach's *B Minor Mass* in the same manner strikes me as less objectionable because Bach's systematic alternation of the text between the two singers seems to me to invite the interpretation I have arrived at. Indeed, being known to attempt to convey theological principles in many other areas of his liturgical music, it seems legitimate to look for messages like this in Bach. In other words, what is *perhaps* a legitimate reading of Beethoven's intentions in his *Gloria* seems much more probable in Bach's equivalent movement; what I would resist is the imposing of a conceptual interpretation upon a piece which cannot be supported by the score.

Two points are of more interest here, though. The first is that Bach, through music, finds a *non-competitive* manner of articulating the Chalcedonian statement that Christ's divine and human natures are to be held together in one man.[86] Indeed, Bach's recognition that this can be done musically leaves one wondering whether any other way of doing so would be as effective. That is, while the messages being taken from these musical examples are conceptual and depend upon the texts being sung (and are therefore not solely dependent upon affective experience, although they are not entirely separable from it either),[87] they cannot

---

[83] Mellers, 1983, p. 305.   [84] Ibid.   [85] Ibid., p. 310.

[86] The Chalcedonian statement (451 CE) requires that Christ be 'recognised in two natures, without confusion, without change, without division, without separation'.

[87] Certainly in the case of the Beethoven, were there not such a clear and obvious musical, and therefore affective, difference between the 'heavenly' and 'earthly' realms, I very much doubt that these categories would have been invoked.

be derived from the texts alone; the interpretations being offered are utterly dependent upon how the texts have been set to music. The second, and this is the real reason for citing these particular examples, is that holding the divine and the earthly together is, as we found to be the case for certain Islamic thinkers, presumed to be a problem. As we shall now see, it is also an issue within certain strains of Judaism.

3.3 The Jewish Suspicion of Art

In his novel *My Name Is Asher Lev* and its sequel, *The Gift of Asher Lev*, Jewish novelist Chaim Potok beautifully captures the tension created within a Hasidic family and its wider community in Brooklyn when the titular character, from a young age, develops into a celebrated and influential visual artist. When asked, during an interview, why there was no Jewish tradition in art, Potok replied,

> In the ancient world all art was inextricably linked with paganism, with the gods – you made images of the gods and you wrote dramas for the gods. The Jew, the Israelite, came into the world with an alternative reading of reality. His was a world not bound by the nature-deities and he loathed the image-making activity of man. Since all of drama and all of graphic creativity was involved with the gods the Jew backed away from that and funnelled all of his creative energy into the one area of human expression where image-making was not three-dimensional – words.
>
> Once image-making became stripped of its relationship to the gods, the Jew began to enter that arena of creativity as well, but that has happened relatively recently in human history because of the connection of the graphic arts to pagan reality.

It might be noted, of course, that the tension Potok describes between image and word echoes the concerns of *Moses und Aron*. And further resonances of Schoenberg's opera can be detected as Potok continues to describe the break with the pagan world that monotheism introduced:

> Jewish civilisation came into the world at war with the nature cycle to which pagan reality was bound and it broke the cyclical grip that nature had on human experience – the gods live, the gods die, the gods are resurrected, they live, die ... that is what man participated in and it was with this that the Jew broke, making God as he saw it beyond the nature cycle, freeing man so that he could create a new world, a new reality with a dream for the future rather than nothing but this endless cyclical trap in which pagan man found himself and the ancient world.[88]

---

[88] In D. Walden (ed.), *Conversations with Chaim Potok* (Jackson: University of Mississippi Press, 2001), pp. 29–30. Potok later makes a similar comment about fiction, which is perhaps surprising given the large number of influential writers who have been Jewish or of Jewish descent: 'There is something in the Jewish tradition which casts a very definite denigrating eye upon the whole

This provides some intellectual and religious context for the story of Asher Lev who, as a young boy, struggles with the discovery of his talent and what place it should occupy within his life as a Torah-observant Hasidic Jew, at one early point temporarily abandoning drawing on the grounds that it is from the *sitra achra* (the 'other side').[89] But despite not being understood by his family, the young Asher is encouraged by their local Rebbe and is articled to a professional artist and sculptor who teaches him the craft and philosophy of being an artist. Asher's conversations with his mentor as well as the apologetic he enters into with his family and community constitute a wonderfully skilful and deeply searching meditation on the meaning of art within a religious context.

For his family and community, art is either a frivolous distraction from study of Torah and meaningful action in the world or it is outright idolatry, but Asher points out that 'The Ten Commandments forbid the worshipping of pictures, not the making of them'.[90] This connects to that judgement in *Moses und Aron* that it is the worshipping of *false* images which is idolatrous, in failing to recognise that all images point to God. On this point, Asher Lev quotes from Cezanne that

> . . . artistic perception had to overcome itself to the point of realising that even something horrible, something that seems no more than disgusting, *is*, and shares the truth of its being with everything else that exists. Just as the creative artist is not allowed to choose, neither is he permitted to turn his back on anything: a single refusal, and he is cast out of the state of grace and becomes sinful all the way through.[91]

In other words, everything participates in beauty by dint of the fact that it *exists*, that it is an intended part of God's Creation. Sinfulness consists in the failure to recognise beauty in everything and in the failure to recognise that its beauty comes from its being created by God. But what the artist teaches us is that the capacity to recognise God as the invisible in the visible requires an alertness and an openness, a receptivity to God's Creation and to the possibility that His communication to us does not consist solely in what is written in Scripture. As Asher reads, when he discovers a book written by the grandfather of his sympathetic Rebbe,

> Even the most unlearned of men knows that the truly important matters of life are those for which we have no words. Yet we must speak of them. We speak, as it were, around them, under them, through them, but not directly of them.

---

enterprise of fiction [. . .] Scholarship is what counts in the Jewish tradition, Talmudic scholarship, not the product of the imagination. That was always frowned upon because it was a menace. The imagination is boundless. It knows no rules and regulations. It is outside the pale of the rational. Rabbinic Judaism of the Talmud is rational; it is bound by the mind and is suspicious of the imagination. Imagination is pagan; imagination is Greek.' p. 36, cf. p. 76 where Potok comments upon Maimonides' 'mistrust of the imagination'.

[89] C. Potok, *My Name Is Asher Lev* (London: Penguin Books, 1973), p. 50.

[90] C. Potok, *The Gift of Asher Lev* (New York: Fawcett Books, 1990), p. 48.   [91] Ibid., p. 178.

Perhaps the Master of the Universe thought it best not to give us those words, for to possess them is to comprehend the awesome mysteries of creation and death, and such comprehension might well make life impossible for us. Hence in His infinite wisdom and compassion the Master of the Universe gave us the obscure riddle rather than the revealing word. Thus we should give thanks to Him and bless His name.[92]

In his interviews, Potok initially appears curiously self-contradictory on this matter, given that he was a visual artist as well as a novelist, once claiming that ' . . . nothing is capable of being understood except through words. Clearly the only way we can communicate is through words'.[93] And when later asked if revelation is attained linguistically or silently, Potok replied that 'Revelation is always attained linguistically. In other words, the content of revelation is words, and words contain the essence of the revelation'. However, he then went on to comment that

There's a silence between the Jewish people, or indeed all religious people, and God in this century. But whatever it is – and I don't understand it – the silence is not a break in communication. It's a communication of a different kind, and what we try to do is tap into it and see what it's all about. *It's very difficult to grasp the notion that silence can be another aspect of the verbal.*[94]

If we combine this comment with my summary of Andrew Bowie in the previous section, what should start to become clear is that there is a *logocentricity* within each of the Abrahamic religions, an emphasis upon language as the medium by which the core tenets of belief are transmitted which, at times, risks precluding the meaning-bearing potential of other media. Now, it is not the purpose of art or music to challenge this entirely because ideas such as monotheism, salvation, the doctrine of creation or the necessity that belief in God should be reflected in one's personal ethics and behaviour require unambiguous communication (if, indeed, that is possible). This is why a religion predicated upon aesthetics alone would be highly questionable and almost certainly would be an incomplete and impoverished way of living out Judaism, Christianity, or Islam.

But what I am trying to articulate is a belief that there are many aspects of quotidian life which are not lived out verbally or conceptually but which are perfectly valid modes of being in the world, and this includes our affective relationship with music. More than this, this non-cognitive relationship to God

---

[92] Ibid., p. 56, cf. p. 93 & 193: 'Truth has to be given in riddles. People can't take truth if it comes charging at them like a bull [. . .] You have to give people the truth in a riddle, hide it so that they go looking for it and find it piece by piece; that way they learn to live with it.'

[93] Interview with Leonard Rubenstein, 1982, *Conversations*, p. 46.

[94] Interview with Elaine M. Kauvar, 1986, *Conversations*, p. 80 (emphasis added).

and the world is *essential*, constituting a form of introspection which is not necessarily egocentric but which recognises that there are aspects of relationship which go beyond words. Even if a painting has identifiable objects which can be described linguistically one can still be hypnotised by it and be unable to put into words what its meaning is but nevertheless continue to find it meaningful. The same can be said for a piece of instrumental music which, as it reaches its end, has communicated much which cannot be contained in words. What is more powerful about all types of art, and indeed any type of encounter, is that they live on in the mind and heart long afterwards and continue to accrue meaningfulness, what George Steiner beautifully describes as 'presence after presentness'.[95] These are valuable analogates for our relationship with God in that they remind us that that relationship cannot be fully understood intellectually but remains deeply meaningful. Indeed, I have tried to argue that it is *because* the relationship cannot be understood intellectually that it is necessary for us because it requires the self-submission which is essential to faith.

3.4 Platonic Philosophy and the Axial Turn

We have nevertheless found in certain strands of Islam, Christianity, and Judaism a presumed gulf between the heavenly and the earthly realms and that a prioritising of the spoken or written word over any other form of communicative media is precisely how the separation should be maintained. Certainly, in what might be taken to be a caricature of certain strands of Christian thought, Søren Kierkegaard,[96] in his essay on Mozart's *Don Giovanni*, argued for the separation, seeing it as a reason to prioritise the intellectual over the sensual:

> As the spirit [reason/intellectual], exclusively specified as spirit, renounces this world, feels that this is not simply not its home but not even its scene of action, and withdraws up into the higher regions, it leaves the worldly behind as the arena for the power with which it has always lived in conflict and for which it now steps aside. As the spirit then frees itself from the world, sensuality appears in all its power; it offers no objection to the

---

[95] G. Steiner, *Real Presences* (Chicago, IL: Chicago University Press, 1989), p. 147.

[96] I describe this as a *possible* caricature because Kierkegaard often used pseudonyms in order to present opposing characters and arguments which makes it difficult to determine whether the views expressed are representative of his own thought, or even if they are to be taken seriously. Alistair McKinnon writes that Kierkegaard 'explicitly disclaimed the views expressed in his pseudonymous works', 'Søren Kierkegaard', in N. Smart, J. Clayton, P. Sherry, & S. Katz (eds.), *Nineteenth Century Religious Thought in the West* (Cambridge: Cambridge University Press, 1985), p. 181, cf. pp. 185–192. Similarly, George Pattison writes that a poetic autobiography should not be extrapolated from Kierkegaard's early works on art, G. Pattison, *Kierkegaard: The Aesthetic and the Religious: From the Magic Theatre to the Crucifixion of the Image* (New York: St Martin's Press, 1992), p. 44.

change, it too sees the advantage in being separated, and rejoices that the Church does not prevail on them to stay together, but hews asunder the bond that binds them.[97]

In keeping with what was suggested during the earlier discussion of Islam, Kierkegaard excludes the aesthetic on ethical grounds, as well as *via* a privileging of the intellectual, the linguistic in particular. And this derives from a dualism between flesh and spirit, supposedly introduced by Christianity.[98] It should perhaps be clear by now that I consider this viewpoint to be quite un-Christian,[99] but it might be helpful to demonstrate that this commonality between the religions has a philosophical complement in Plato and early Classical conceptions of music.

3.5 The Harmony of the Spheres

It was for a long time believed that music could help us attune ourselves to the order of the cosmos and bring about moral improvement within the self. Of course, we are now so accustomed to seeing music in purely human terms that we find it hard to imagine that its powers might connect us to the very mechanisms of the universe and thereby adjoin the individual to the wider order of things. Nevertheless, it was held that the universe itself was ordered, and that its harmony was a musical one. This can be traced back through Plato to Pythagoras' discovery of the Harmonic Series.

The Harmonic Series refers to a Pythagorean experiment that can readily be reproduced in the present day on a guitar or any stringed instrument. If one takes a string which is tightened to a consistent tension and strikes it at certain points, measured mathematically, the string will produce a series of harmonics. So, for example, if one lightly touches the string at its halfway point and plucks it, the harmonic an octave above the open string will sound. If one moves to two thirds, the harmonic an octave and a fifth above the original pitch will be produced, and if one continues this at three quarters, four fifths, and five sixths, one can produce the second octave, and then the intervals of the tenth and twelfth respectively. In other words, following this process produces the notes of a major chord arpeggio which forms the basis of musical harmony. The series continues, but the less pure the ratio the less strong is the harmonic produced.

---

[97] Kierkegaard, p. 97.

[98] For a fuller treatment of Kierkegaard's discussion of Mozart's *Don Giovanni*, see G. Wilson, 'Music, atheism, and modernity: aesthetics, morality, and the theological construction of the self', in J. Hawkey, B. Quash, & V. White (eds.), *God's Song and Music's Meanings: Theology, Liturgy, and Musicology in Dialogue* (Oxon: Routledge, 2020), pp. 63–78.

[99] As Marsh and Roberts write, 'With good biblical precedent, Christianity has often sought to remain detached from "the world," where the world is easily seen as ungodly and sinful. The same bible reminds people of faith that Creation is God's, that humans are made in God's image, and that the world is the object of God's love'. Marsh & Roberts, *Personal Jesus*, p. 31.

The fact that the intervals of the harmonic series are discovered by employing the strictest and purest mathematical ratios demonstrated for some that the universe is *ordered*; if it be accepted that $2 + 2 = 4$ is a statement which is objectively true, then the harmonic series, because it pertains to this type of objectivity, might be held to be representative of a divine order.

Following on from this, the 'Harmony of the Spheres' is the notion that the planets and stars of the universe, by dint of the movement of their different sizes and carefully measured, proportioned distances, generate a cosmic music. By performing or listening to music, the individual could 'tune in' to this heavenly music and participate in its order, thereby achieving order within the self. A link between music and morality was therefore created by virtue of the belief that music was good for the character,[100] re-tuning it to the harmony of the cosmos.[101]

However, while Plato holds that music can calm the emotions and rid the body of passion, it can also do precisely the opposite and create disorder within the soul. As he writes in *Timaeus*:

> [. . .] all audible musical sound is given us for the sake of harmony, which has motions akin to the orbits in our soul, and which, as anyone who makes intelligent use of the arts knows, is not to be used, as is commonly thought, to give irrational pleasure, but as a heaven-sent ally in reducing to order and concord any disharmony that has arisen in the revolutions within us. Rhythm, again, was given us from the same heavenly source to help us in the same way; for most of us lack measure and grace.[102]

For Plato, to be in a correct state of self-control, powered by good use of reason, is to be in right relationship with the natural order;[103] the state of aesthetic euphoria is therefore to be treated with disdain. He is anxious to maintain a balance within the soul which prioritises reason over the emotions and writes that ' . . . These people, then, who are anxious to take part in the finest possible singing, should, apparently, look not for a music which is sweet, but one which

---

[100] '[. . .] rhythm and harmony penetrate deeply into the mind and take a most powerful hold on it, and, if education is good, being and impart grace and beauty, if it is bad, the reverse'. Plato, *Republic*, 400d.

[101] For fuller treatments, cf. D. Chua, *Absolute Music and the Construction of Meaning* (Cambridge: Cambridge University Press, 1999), pp. 12–22. Cf. J. Begbie, *Resounding Truth: Christian Wisdom in the World of Music* (London: SPCK, 2007), pp. 78–83; M. E. Bonds, *Absolute Music: The History of an Idea* (Oxford: Oxford University Press, 2014), pp. 23–29; Bowie, p.33; P. Vergo, *That Divine Order: Music and the Visual Arts from Antiquity to the Eighteenth Century* (London: Phaidon, 2005), pp. 68–79.

[102] Plato, *Timaeus*, tr. D. Lee (London: Penguin Classics, 2008), 47d.

[103] 'So reason can be understood as the perception of the natural or right order, and to be ruled by reason is to be ruled by a vision of this order.' C. Taylor, *Sources of the Self: The Making of the Modern Identity* (Cambridge, MA: Harvard University Press, 1989), p. 121.

is correct'.[104] The assumption, prevalent throughout Plato's *Theory of Art*, is that something's emotive qualities have the potential to undermine its truth.[105] Truth is assumed to be rational, and the harmonic series, by dint of its coinciding with mathematical ratios, underpins this rationality. Thus, the real significance of music lay in the study of ratios, not in the practical performance of music which was held only to reach the surface of what music really embodies. As we found in Schopenhauer, for whom Plato was an acknowledged influence, the belief that everything on earth is a mere copy of a truer metaphysical prototype results in a certain anti-materialism, a denigration of the physical.

This separation between the heavenly and the earthly which manifests itself in mind/body, spirit/matter dualisms and which we have found in certain conceptions of Judaism, Christianity, and Islam, is known as the 'Axial turn' which, according to Donald Wehrs, arrived with Plato (the pre-Axial period having been influenced by belief in the Greek gods and by the fact that, as anthropomorphic figures, the worldly and the heavenly were conjoined in them and the dichotomies of mind/body or spirit/matter did not obtain – we can recognise much of this in Chaim Potok's comment earlier).[106] But these dualisms also result, in Plato, in an inner/outer dichotomy whereby the private and the public become separated. What is striking when one reads Plato's *Theory of Art*, particularly in his denunciation of poetry and tragic drama, is that empathy for others, which watching encourages, is actively to be resisted. Claiming that it is easy for the poet to represent a character who is 'unstable and refractory',[107] Plato writes of how easily the audience is encouraged to indulge in their feelings for the tragic hero.[108] He then writes that

> [...] very few people are capable of realising that what we feel for other people must infect what we feel for ourselves, and that if we let our pity for the misfortunes of others grow too strong it will be difficult to restrain our feelings in our own.[109]

Donald Wehrs thus claims that the internal affects aroused by poetry are troublesome to Plato not simply because they incite emotional indulgence and elevate worldly values, but also because they distract us from the self-control which comes from contemplating *the real*. He therefore writes that 'Poetry's

---

[104] Plato, *Laws*, tr. T. J. Saunders (London: Penguin Classics, 1970), 668b.

[105] Plato, 'Theory of Art', *The Republic*, part X.

[106] Donald Wehrs, 'Introduction: Affect and Texts: Contemporary Inquiry in Historical Context', D. R. Wehrs, & T. Blake (ed.), *The Palgrave Handbook of Affect Studies and Textual Criticism* (Cham: Palgrave MacMillan, 2017), p.6.

[107] Plato, *Republic*, 605a.   [108] Ibid., 605d.

[109] Ibid., 606b. Plato thus concludes that '[...] bad taste in the theatre may insensibly lead you into becoming a buffoon at home'. 606c.

making us forget ourselves in feeling for another, by contrast, takes us out of our wits or senses [. . .] Direct access to the real through reason cleanses mimesis of affective disturbance and distortion'.[110]

Aristotle, however, argued for a more symbiotic relationship between reason and emotion and recognised the benefits of humans imitating each other because this is precisely how children learn to become adults. This, in turn, resulted in a more appreciative account of poetry. As he writes in the *Poetics*:

> Imitation comes naturally to human beings from childhood (and in this they differ from other animals, i.e., in having a strong propensity to imitation and in learning their earliest lessons through imitation) [. . .] This is the reason why people take delight in seeing images; what happens is that as they view them they come to understand and work out what each thing is (e.g. 'This is so-and-so').[111]

For Aristotle, then, humans flourish through interaction with each other which is why they are interested in the potential models presented by dramatic poetry. He thereby connected intellect and emotion with morality and sociability. As Wehrs writes, '[Aristotle] linked body and soul, nature and nurture, in ways that anticipate twenty-first century inquiry and offered rational defenses of seemingly "archaic" experiencing and conceptualising of human life [i.e., the pre-Axial]'.[112] There is certainly something in Aristotle's conception of things which should resonate with the demand in Abrahamic monotheism for moral action resulting from empathy for others; there is some version in each of the Abrahamic faiths of the requirement to make God's presence known to others precisely through interaction of every type. But this must surely result from a deep-seated realisation that God and world are *not* separate, that God makes Himself known to the world through self-revelation in Torah, Christ, Qur'an and through Creation itself, that God imbues the world with connectedness.

What is deeply telling is that the editorial commentary to Plato's *Theory of Art* includes a brief quotation from Leo Tolstoy's *What is Art?* which defines art as *communication*. As Tolstoy writes, 'Art is a human activity, consisting in this, that one man consciously, by means of certain external signs, hands on to others the feelings he has lived through, and that other people are infected by these feelings, and also experience them'. The commentary continues,

---

[110] Wehrs, p. 6.

[111] Aristotle, *Poetics*, tr. M. Heath (London: Penguin Books, 1996), 3.2. Aristotle continues, 'Given, then, that imitation is natural to us, and also melody and rhythm (it being obvious that verse-forms are segments of rhythm), from the beginning those who had the strongest natural inclination towards these things generated poetry out of improvised activities by a process of gradual innovation'.

[112] Wehrs, p. 8.

> Both Plato and Tolstoy think that the poet and artist in some way *infect* those who read or see their productions with the feelings which those productions portray, and since the feelings portrayed are often morally questionable, such portrayal must be treated with the greatest caution.[113]

This comment betrays certain assumptions which are open to challenge. The first is that Plato and Tolstoy assume uniformity of subjective perception. For Plato, this might be a corollary of his belief in a unified order, participation in which results in rightness of reason. But I have been arguing that music needs to be seen in more subjective terms, where individual context is paramount and where objectivity of perception is considered unobtainable. This is demonstrated by the *Wozzeck* experiment I related in my Introduction and is reflected by the philosophy/theology of music I have been proposing.

The second assumption at play is that of artistic intentionality, that art obeys the intentions of the artist rather than dictating its own form to him or her. It would be too much of a digression to respond to this here as fully as I might like, but there is a groundswell of artistic opinion (including such names as Fyodor Dostoevsky, David Jones, T. S. Eliot, and Flannery O'Connor as well as Catholic theologian Jacques Maritain) which denies that the artist's intentions are sovereign. As Rowan Williams puts it,

> art, [. . .] can't properly begin with a message and then seek for a vehicle. Its roots lie, rather, in the single story or metaphor or configuration of sound or shape which *requires* attention and development from the artist. In the process of that development, we find meanings we had not suspected; but if we try to begin with the meanings, they will shrink to the scale of what we already understand; whereas creative activity opens up what we did not understand and perhaps will not fully understand even when the actual work of creation is done. That is why the artist is never the sole or even the best judge of the work, which rightly and properly escapes into the interpretative field of its public.[114]

Both of these points are important as responses to attempts on the part of any religion to impose censures on particular pieces or types of music; we cannot

---

[113] Melissa Lane, Commentary on *The Republic*, p. 352, emphasis original.

[114] Rowan Williams, 'Making it Strange: Theology in Other(s') Words', in J. Begbie (ed.), *Sounding the Depths* (London: SCM Press, 2002), p. 28. Flannery O'Connor puts it more succinctly: 'You don't dream up a form and put the truth in it. The truth creates its own form.' S. Fitzgerald (ed.), *Letters of Flannery O'Connor: The Habit of Being* (New York: Farrar, Strauss & Giroux, 1979), p. 218. In *Mystery & Manners*, O'Connor writes, 'In most good stories it is the character's personality that creates the action of the story [. . .] If you start with a real personality, a real character, then something is bound to happen; and you don't have to know what before you begin. You ought to be able to discover something from your stories. If you don't, probably nobody else will'. Augustine, *Mystery & Manners* (London: Faber & Faber, 1972), pp. 105–106.

guarantee that all will respond to the same piece in the same way, and not even the composer is in a position to dictate how the piece should be received.

But the most important assumption arising from Tolstoy, which I would wholeheartedly wish to uphold, is that art is *communicative* and it is communication itself which, I believe, is the key concept for a theology of art or music. If we can agree with Tolstoy that art in its many forms is communication (even if we need not agree about *what* is being communicated) and if it is accepted by Jews, Christians, and Muslims, that Creation (by which I mean the universe and everything within it) is God's communication of Himself, then Creation itself is divine art – physical, visual, textural, sensual, and sonic; intended to speak to all of the human senses. The idea of a separation between God and world is thus very far from what Abrahamic monotheism seeks to uphold.

Aristotle's rehabilitation of poetry is therefore important not just because it resists the worldly/heavenly dichotomy which Plato upholds and which we find in much Abrahamic monotheism. It also finds support in present-day affect theory (as well as in some theology) which argues that reason which is uninfluenced by emotion is faulty, that emotion gives rational judgement a sense of purpose and urgency and that reciprocity between the two is essential for mature personhood.[115] Moreover, it denies the mind/body dualism to which Plato's philosophy might lead and seeks to integrate the human person, connecting the emotions with the intellect, the mental with the physical, and the spiritual with the worldly, the world which God has created and with which He seeks to communicate.

4 Knowing the Unknowable God?

> The only thing that gives meaning is what doesn't mean anything in the normal sense.
>
> Jon Fosse, *A New Name*

In the previous section I wrote that objects participate in beauty by virtue of their very existence and that the failure to recognise beauty in everything is a spiritual one because createdness comes from God. I therefore emphasised the importance of an openness to God's Creation and suggested the possibility that His communication to us need not consist solely in what is written in Scripture, that the Word of God may not be reducible to the text of God.[116] And if it is

---

[115] Wehrs, pp. 2–3, cf. R. C. Sha, 'The Turn to Affect: Emotions without Subjects, Causality without Demonstrable Cause', *Palgrave Handbook*, pp. 259–278.

[116] This finds support in certain strands of Sufi mysticism, as Hazrat Inayat Khan writes, 'There is nothing in the world which is not the instrument of God [. . .] A Sufi must always recognise in God the source of all things and the origin of all beings'. Hazrat Inayat Khan, *The Mysticism of Sound and Music: The Sufi Teaching of Hazrat Inayat Khan* (Boulder, CO: Shambhala, 1991), pp. 116–117.

accepted that monotheism results in the understanding that language is unable to contain God but that relationship between God and His creation nevertheless obtains, it will become necessary to ask whether He will provide non-linguistic signs of His goodness within Creation.

4.1 Islam and Signs of God in the World

Celene Ibrahim writes about the Islamic emphasis upon God's signs in the world, both in what is exterior to the human person and in what resides within.[117] Indeed, arguing that the Qur'an contains some 350 verses referencing the concept of God's signs in Creation, Ibrahim writes that

> The Qur'an [...] stresses that signs contained in the unfolding of human history are apparent to those who make the required effort to discern them. Even ways in which human beings manipulate their natural world to derive benefit (e.g., food, clothing, transportation, shelter, and so forth) are regarded as signs of God's benevolence.[118]

Yet she links this with the Islamic belief that strict adherence to monotheism is what keeps the Muslim on the true and correct path. So while there is undoubtedly the danger that one can be distracted from contemplation of the divine by things within Creation (and we have already recounted forms of this concern in all three religions under discussion), ignoring God's signs within Creation might be just as dangerous. In other words, there is not competition but *complementarity* between contemplation of God and reflection upon signs of His intimacy with the world.[119]

This can be connected to Saint Augustine's adoption of Plato's argument, expounded in the previous section, that reason is inherent in the external order of the cosmos. Augustine took this further by equating the Platonic Ideas or Forms with the thoughts (or Word) of God as expressed in Creation and Christ; everything in Creation, for Augustine, expresses God's mind and thereby signals his presence.[120] But Augustine made the conversion to interiority by interpreting Plato's dichotomy of spirit/matter in terms of inner/outer, thereby establishing another dualism.[121] What interested Augustine most, however, was not *what* we could know, but *that* we could know and, further, that we can witness our own act of knowing.[122] This 'radical reflexivity', that is, our being

---

[117] Ibrahim, p. 18.   [118] Ibrahim, p. 18.

[119] 'According to the Islamic understanding, *tawḥīd* is grasped through the innate human disposition and through observation and contemplation of the signs that God has placed in the world. *Tawḥīd* is discerned when human beings contemplate these signs – natural phenomena and the wonders of their being itself [...] Introspection and observation of the cosmos point a person of upright character and understanding toward the creed of pure monotheism.' Ibrahim, p. 48.

[120] C. Taylor, *Sources of the Self* (Cambridge, MA: Harvard University Press, 1989), p. 128.

[121] Ibid., p. 129.   [122] Ibid., p. 130.

aware of our own awareness, of our witnessing our own receptivity to things, elevates the aesthetic as an aid to our recognition of the very act of experiencing, and Augustine considered its 'drawing inward-ness' a channel to God.

There is therefore a connection between the heaven/earth dichotomy, versions of which can be found in all three Abrahamic religions, and the mind/body dualism which has occupied much philosophical thought throughout the Modern period. However, a recurring theme in present-day affect theory is the recognition that attending properly to our aesthetic response helps rid us of this dualism. Florian Cova, Julien Deonna, and David Sander write,

> If [. . .] appreciation of sad works of art is tied to the activity of reflecting on meaningful questions about the human condition, then we should conclude that feelings of being moved have an intimate link with this kind of contemplation, and that eudaimonic gratification is best understood as a blend of cognitive activity (reflecting on meaningful questions) and affective states (feelings of being moved).[123]

Similarly, Richard Sha writes that '[. . .] emotion and imagination become parts of reflection, and thus become additional resources beyond rationality to be exploited [. . .] One simply has to recognise that reflection is not limited to rationality and that one can reflect upon emotion'.[124] In other words, cognition *is* emotional, and reflecting upon the fact that we have become emotional requires cognitive activity. The implosion of this dualism of the intellectual and the physical is of import for this enquiry because it has some bearing upon the place of the aesthetic within religious life, and what I am arguing is that what might be taken to be a prioritising of the affective or the aesthetic over the semantic in fact signals a confluence between the two.

It will be remembered that, in Islam, melodic recitation of text, whether Qur'anic or otherwise, was held to be a greater means of internalising the word, that the combination of text with melody increases our apprehension and remembrance of it thereby blurring the boundary between the semantic and the aesthetic, if, indeed, that boundary exists. If the power and truth of a symbol consists in its ability to point to God, then, we will be required to have a more nuanced understanding of our receptivity than one which simply associates factual statements with literal meaning and non-factual statements with the symbolic. For example, while many find the metaphor 'God is a rock' meaningful, no monotheist should believe that God is literally a rock. Instead,

---

[123] Cova, Deonna, & Sander, p. 356. Cf. R. Sha, 'When distance is framed not as negation of feeling but rather as being enabled by feeling, rationality and the passions need have no necessary antagonism'. R. C. Sha, 'The Turn to Affect: Emotions without Subjects, Causality without Demonstrable Cause', *Palgrave*, p. 270.

[124] Sha, p. 271.

I propose that this metaphor is an instance of genuine complementarity between the semantic and the aesthetic, of using what we can say about a rock as a means of knowing the unknowable God.

The erosion of the mind/body dualism also results from the doctrine of Creation that Abrahamic monotheism upholds. In *Mystery and Manners*, Flannery O'Connor writes that 'Fiction operates through the senses [. . .] The first and most obvious characteristic of fiction is that it deals with reality through what can be seen, heard, smelt, tasted, and touched'.[125] Creation is God's medium for communication (it is the medium in which Torah, Christ, and Qur'an are received) and it is the arena in which we, by virtue of the human senses, are recipients of His divine address. This means that how we construe our place in God's Creation is fundamental to our understanding of our relationship to God Himself. And what I am arguing for here is that a sense of embeddedness in God's Creation, both intellectually and affectively, must be facilitated by our receptivity to it. Anything which stimulates our receptivity, then, must be of significance for religious faith.

In his attempt to define mysticism, Gershon Scholem points to the Thomistic understanding as '*cognitio dei experimentalis*; the knowledge of God through experience', and that the task of the mystic as well as the theologian is to identify the essence of this experience.[126] For Scholem the heaven/earth dichotomy is a logical consequence of monotheism, that Abrahamic religion creates an absolute abyss between the transcendent and the creaturely which can be bridged only by the voice of God in revelation and the voice of humanity through prayer.[127] But revelation need not be construed solely as a *Deus ex machina* rupture of our regular mode of experience. If what I have been arguing here has theological purchase, that being receptive to God's signs in and through Creation sustains us in relationship with Him, revelation can instead be understood as something more continuous in its nature. As Scholem writes,

> [Revelation is] not only a definite historical occurrence which, at a given moment in history puts an end to any further direct relation between mankind and God. With no thought of denying Revelation as a fact of history, the mystic still conceives the source of religious knowledge and experience which bursts forth from his own heart as being of equal importance for the conception of religious truth. In other words, instead of the one act of Revelation, there is a constant repetition of this act [. . .] hence the new interpretation given to canonical texts and sacred books of the great religions.[128]

---

[125] F. O'Connor, *Mystery and Manners*, p. 91. In his Introduction to David Jones' *In Parenthesis*, T. S. Eliot concludes that 'Understanding begins in the sensibility'. D. Jones, *In Parenthesis* (London: Faber & Faber, 1961), p. viii.

[126] G. Scholem, *Major Trends in Jewish Mysticism* (New York: Schocken Books, 1974), p. 4.

[127] Ibid., p. 8.   [128] Ibid., p. 9.

This is why what I have been writing about is not a high-level mysticism such as that found in Kabbalism or Sufism (not that I intend any disrespect to these traditions). I have instead set my sights rather lower by trying to recognise the inherent and substantial spiritual power of ordinary quotidian experience. I have sought to argue that music, and indeed all of the arts, point to something wondrous about human existence, imagination, connectivity, communicability, and receptivity, and that they remind us to recognise and be more attentive to our divinely given surroundings, enabling us to submit to that which we do not necessarily understand or control, namely, the sacred.

4.2 The *Sensus Communis*

Furthermore, Islam's notion of openness to God's signs in the world (which finds complementarities in Christianity and Judaism), the recognition that every being's quiddity or createdness points to its being desired by God by dint of Abrahamic monotheism's shared doctrine of Creation, is a means by which commonality between the faiths can be reached: what people of faith have in common, despite their many differences, is a receptivity to that which is other than themselves. As Lutheran theologian Friedrich Schleiermacher holds, unity is achieved through the acknowledgement of the capacity for sensual perception common to all.

> If unlimited universality of sense is the first and most original condition of religion, and is therefore naturally also its most beautiful and ripest fruit, you can surely see that nothing else is feasible than that the further you progress in religion the more the whole religious world must appear to you as an indivisible whole.[129]

In other words, our shared capacity for aesthetic perception, our *sensus communis*, unites us; although what we intuit must necessarily differ, the very fact of perception provides commonality between individuals. We can be receptive to divine beauty and participate in God's delight in it, but Schleiermacher makes us aware that we join with others simply by engaging our shared aesthetic sensibilities. This is the type of universality which I believe can legitimately be argued for despite the recognition that that to which we are receptive might differ dramatically. Although Gershom Scholem writes that 'There is no mysticism as such, there is only the mysticism of a particular religious system, Christian, Islamic, Jewish mysticism and so on', he goes on to concede, 'That there remains a common characteristic it would be absurd to deny, and it is this element which is brought out in the comparative analysis of particular mystical experiences'.[130] Thus, when

---

[129] F. Schleiermacher, *On Religion: Speeches to Its Cultured Despisers*, tr. R. Crouter (Cambridge: Cambridge University Press, 2008), pp. 76–77.

[130] Scholem, p. 6.

Hazrat Inayat Khan writes that 'It would be no exaggeration if I said that music alone can be the means by which the souls of races, nations and families, which are today so apart, may one day be united', he need not be taken to mean that the same *kind* of music will draw us together. We might each enjoy something different but our capacity for aesthetic enjoyment itself remains the commonality.[131] As Khan continues, 'As to the law of music which exists in different nations, there are of course different methods, but in the conception of beauty there is no difference'.[132] This is the sense in which I would like to claim that music is a universal language, not that one kind of music will appeal to all, or that one form of musical language is superior to others, but that music's communicability is cross-cultural because communicability itself is universal and, moreover, is divinely willed.

4.3 Affect Theory and Aesthetic Unpredictability

Khan, however, appears to press further by arguing for the type of musical universalism from which I have shied away. He writes,

> Suppose a man comes from the far East, the extreme North, South, or West; wherever he sees the beauty of nature he cannot help but admire and love it. So it is with the music lover. From whatever country he comes, and whatever music he hears, if the music has a soul, and if he seeks for the soul in music, he will appreciate and admire all music.[133]

This may or may not be true, but what is of more interest is how it is decided that a piece of music has a soul or not. Earlier, I alluded to the question of how sacred music can be distinguished from secular music and suggested that the distinction is often made without sufficient musical justification.[134] Indeed, I would venture to suggest that the distinction cannot be made at all. But here, drawing upon support from various affect theorists, I would like to establish further just how elusive music is as a medium and how mysterious and unpredictable its powers are, and this maps onto what exactly is meant by affect, emotion, or 'the aesthetic'. On the

---

[131] Khan, p. 7.   [132] Ibid.   [133] Ibid.

[134] For example, in the (otherwise profoundly instructive) aesthetic theology of Jacques Maritain, certain elements of Richard Wagner's ('secular') music are deemed offensive, but Maritain never specifies exactly which musical features are objectionable or why; if the 'gigantism' of *Parsifal* refers to its length and volume one might enquire why the length of Bach's *St Matthew Passion* or the triumphalism of his *B Minor Mass* escape censure. He claims that Igor Stravinsky's post-*Rite of Spring* work successfully characterises 'strict classical "austerity"', without explaining why, and never identifies what, specifically, 'debauches' the eye, ear, or mind, thereby demonstrating the difficulty of formulating judgements which are not, ultimately, arbitrary. Part of what I am concerned to argue is that dismissing certain types of music without sufficient justification risks restricting art's communicative scope. J. Maritain, *Art and Scholasticism*, tr. B. Barbour (Tacoma, WA: Cluny Media, 2016), p. 60.

one hand, it might appear unsatisfactory to assume that these terms can be treated interchangeably. On the other, there seems to be little agreement as to how they might be delineated. In the Introduction to *Affect Theory Reader*, Melissa Greig and Greg Seigworth write, 'There is no single, generalisable theory of affect: not yet, and (thankfully) there never will be', and continue, 'Because affect emerges out of muddy, unmediated relatedness and not in some dialectical reconciliation of cleanly oppositional elements or primary units, it makes easy compartmentalisms give way to thresholds and tensions, blends and blurs'.[135] Karen Bray and Stephen Moore make the connection between this indefinability and theology: '*Affectivity*, it seems, is no less elusive a concept than *divinity*. It slides, it shifts, it shimmers. Yet its serpentine, often subterranean, movements are anything but immaterial [...] It has affinity with divinity, but a divinity that is indissociable from materiality.'[136] The last part of this comment is significant for my enquiry because it speaks to the nature of religious experience for which I have been arguing, namely one which is embedded within Creation. As Bray and Moore continue, 'The divinity with which affectivity is intimate dwells particularly in the mundane, the quotidian, the humdrum. Affectivity is always incarnate'.[137] Creation is the medium of divine revelation which means that Creation's ordinariness, for which I have been argu-ing, is also miraculous, and it is through our own carnal, somatic sensibility that we are receptive to it. Given that music can only be experienced within Creation, then, it must be held to constitute part of God's communication of Himself to the world. But I would also wish to reiterate that a striking affective moment can obtain within the ordinary, that it need not necessarily arrive during the highest periods of mystical worship in the synagogue, mosque, or chapel. Such a moment might instead arrive while performing mundane tasks in the home, or while driving a car, being in a shopping centre or restaurant. As Cecilia Sjöholm writes,

> What brings affects and emotions together is not their quality, origin, or function. It is their way of affecting the subject [... René] Descartes deployed the word 'affectus' for passion. But the passions are not to be regarded as physiological or psychological experiences of a certain class. They are said to be 'all sorts of cases of perception or knowledge to be found in us'. What connects these phenomena is the way in which they simply seem to hit us, beyond our will-power.[138]

---

[135] M. Gregg, & G. J. Seigworth (eds.), *The Affect Theory Reader* (Durham & London: Duke University Press, 2010), pp. 3–4.
[136] K. Bray, & S. D. Moore (eds.), *Religion, Emotion, Sensation: Affect Theories and Theologies* (New York: Fordham University Press, 2020), p. 1.
[137] Ibid.
[138] C. Sjöholm, 'Descartes, Emotions and the Inner Life of the Subject', *Palgrave Handbook*, p. 655.

Not only is affectivity difficult to define, then, its arrival is also impossible to predict. In observing that one can just as easily be transported by a piece of *kitsch* as by an acknowledged masterwork, George Steiner recognises that we do not *choose* that to which we respond.[139] In the same vein, Marsh and Roberts write that 'Profound things could happen to a person in interaction with a television melodrama or a (musically) poor pop song'.[140] I recognise from my own experience that I might respond immediately to one piece of music and not another, and although I can identify the specific features which make a piece of music instantly attractive to me, these same features might be found in another piece which takes longer to make an affective impression. Moreover, I cannot say *why* I find myself drawn to these features. As Schopenhauer understood so profoundly, while I can choose my preferences, what I prefer is not in my control.[141]

It is generally conceded by affect theorists that the field has made no progress in being able to account for this. As Sloboda and Juslin comment, 'It is now indisputable that people feel real emotions (rather than simply observing or inferring them) while listening to music, and that specific features of the music have a causal role in such emotions. On the other hand [...] it is impossible to predict what emotion a person may feel solely from the musical content'.[142] This means that while music defies understanding it is also resistant to manipulation and cannot be deployed in order to stimulate one singular affect among its audience. How, then, can it be decided that certain types of music are appropriate for religious usage while others should be forbidden on the grounds that they will incite immorality if music's affective power is so manifestly unquantifiable? How do we determine whether an instrumental piece of music can be described as 'sacred'?

More importantly, have we now established any grounds for wondering whether the act of listening to music can be described as a religious act regardless of whether the listener explicitly thematises the experience as

---

[139] Steiner, pp. 153–154.   [140] Marsh & Roberts, p. 17.

[141] Schopenhauer, *Prize Essay on the Freedom of the Will*, pp. 19–21.

[142] P. N. Juslin, & J. A. Sloboda (eds.), *Handbook of Music & Emotion: Theory, Research, Applications* (Oxford: Oxford University Press, 2010), p. 91. In *The Affect Theory Reader*, Greig and Seigworth write, 'This promise of affect and its generative relay into affect theory must acknowledge [...] that there are no ultimate or final guarantees [...] that capacities to affect and to be affected will yield an actualised next or new that is somehow better than "now." Such seeming moments of promise can just as readily come to deliver something worse' (pp. 9–10). Stephen Davies writes, 'Musical features ground music's expressiveness, and it is interesting to discover what those features are, but identifying them is, at best, only an initial step toward an informative theory of musical expressiveness'. S. Davies, 'Emotions expressed and aroused by music: philosophical perspectives', *Handbook of Music & Emotion*, p.24; Sjöholm, 'Whereas Music Can Be Used to Evoke Certain Moods, Its Effects Are Individual', *Palgrave*, p.660.

such? As Marsh and Roberts write, 'No matter how the term "spirituality" is used, it is difficult to dispute that some form of inner life is being acknowledged and cultivated by engaged, sustained listening, whether or not the listener is explicitly religious'.[143] If we accept that God is communicative, that Creation is His act of communication and that we are His intended recipients of that act, then we are built to be receptive. The question I would like to put, therefore, is this: by being receptive to God's Creation and the innumerable communicative (or musical) acts therein, both His and ours, are we in some way participating in God's relationship with humanity whether we know it or not? Because I have no right to speak to those outside of my own faith tradition I feel obligated to leave this question as a question. My hope, however, is that I have provided enough reason to suggest that it is a question which deserves to be asked.

5 Telling All the Truth?

> Tell all the truth but tell it slant —
> Success in Circuit lies
> Too bright for our infirm Delight
> The Truth's superb surprise
> As Lightning to the Children eased
> With explanation kind
> The Truth must dazzle gradually
> Or every man be blind. (Emily Dickinson)

In the preceding sections I have drawn upon various strands within Abrahamic monotheism, as well as secular philosophy and affect theory, to argue for a generous theological estimate of human aesthetic enjoyment. Given the doctrine of Creation which monotheism necessarily entails, I have argued that everything in the world, by dint of its createdness, in some way points to its Creator. I have suggested that music's 'formlessness' or lack of conceptual clarity is not only a helpful analogate for God's irreducibility but that the removal of semantic control which it enjoins is instructive for the life of faith. I have asked how significant it is for the human relationship to God and the world that we find musical experience meaningful and have even questioned whether music must be recognisably and explicitly 'sacred' in order to place us in relationship with the divine.

But to take some religious objections to music more seriously it is important to emphasise that they are not unjustified. In *Bach's Dialogue With Modernity*, John Butt writes that 'The particular threat to the religious function of [. . .] music lies in the degree to which it is successful in representing, and even embodying, considerable levels of subjectivity; in this way it gains the potential

---

[143] Marsh & Roberts, *Personal Jesus*, p. 136.

to be detached from its quite specific devotional targets'.[144] In other words, as we have seen in Judaism, Christianity, Islam, and Platonism, and are repeatedly reminded throughout Schoenberg's *Moses und Aron*, worldly phenomena (including music) have the capacity to direct the self towards something other than God. And what is notable in Butt's comment is the implied connection between idolatry and subjectivity, that, as I suggested at the end of Section 2, the real idolatry is that of the self.

Faith in God, however conceived, requires submission of the self to the divine, and while Schleiermacher's emphasis on the aesthetic aspects to religion and his positing of a *sensus communis* is of extreme value, it would be unwise to proffer a religion which underemphasises its credal aspects. For if there is no demand for self-submission through faith in certain claims, however interpreted, it is hard to see how it can be adequately transformative. While each person's religion must be different insofar as all are unique, if scripture and doctrine are jettisoned there is nothing to prevent individuals from indulging personal fictions.

And while a turning from the heavenly/earthly dichotomy and subsequent focus upon our place within Creation is to be welcomed, its corollary is the risk that the heavenly is forgotten altogether. Furthermore, and this is yet more unfortunate, the inner/outer dualism can remain. As Charles Taylor writes,

> [Augustine's inward turn] was a fateful one, because we have certainly made a big thing of the first-person standpoint. The modern epistemological tradition from Descartes, and all that has flowed from it in modern culture, has made this standpoint fundamental [...] It has gone as far as generating the view that there is a special domain of 'inner' objects available only from this standpoint; or the notion that the vantage point of the 'I think' is somehow outside the world of things we experience.[145]

In other words, the Aristotelian quest to find 'the real' in the earthly has resulted in a subsequent turning from Creation in favour of the self; the danger of undermining belief in the cosmic order is that if one no longer attains self-mastery by aligning oneself with the cosmos one seeks other means. Scientific knowledge therefore becomes paramount; the more correctly one apprehends outer reality, the firmer one's grasp of truth becomes, the external being objectified *via* the mind and juxtaposed with inner spirit thereby solidifying an inner/outer dichotomy.[146] This means that Creation is regarded less reverently as the self is prioritised. Taylor writes,

---

[144] J. Butt, *Bach's Dialogue with Modernity* (Cambridge: Cambridge University Press, 2010), p. 95.

[145] Taylor, p. 131.

[146] 'Coming to a full realisation of one's being as immaterial involves perceiving distinctly the ontological cleft between the two, and this involves grasping the material world as mere extension.' Taylor, p. 145.

We have to stop thinking of matter as the locus of events and qualities whose true nature is mental. And we do this by objectifying it, that is, by understanding it as 'disenchanted', as mere mechanism, devoid of any spiritual essence or expressive dimension [...] If we follow this line, then the self-mastery of reason now must consist in this capacity being the controlling element in our lives.[147]

Separating the earthly from the heavenly was therefore a catalyst for the onset of individualism; if self-mastery is paramount and is indicated by being in control of one's passions, humanity presumes to become the source of its *own* moral strength. Control of the self is also considered a prerequisite for freewill which '[...] makes us in a certain manner equal to God and exempts us from being His subjects'.[148] Self-control, then, is how the process of internalisation results in the autonomous self and self-idolatry.

I would not attribute these God-denying movements to any one theological or philosophical gesture, however. I would instead propose that humanity is, by nature, self-interested. We have seen that this was appreciated by Plato but it is clearly recognised by all three Abrahamic religions, regardless of whether they share a belief in human fallenness. But we cannot ignore human history and return to the Platonic world view. We must find other ways of respecting God's otherness without succumbing to the paralysis of Schoenberg's Moses.

And while recognising humanity's brokenness is why all three religions emphasise ritual, communal worship, sacrament, and scripture, all of which are means of connecting and re-connecting with the divine, if we do not place *all* human experience within the context of the divine we risk re-establishing the separation between the sacred and the secular. As Raymond Pannikar writes, 'Who are we to limit the works of God, or to prescribe to Him what He has to do?'[149] Indeed, who are we to dictate where God's signs in the world are to be found? Who are we to determine that His presence cannot be signalled by a work of art or a piece of music simply because He is not explicitly addressed within it? Respecting the inexplicability of interiorised aesthetic experience might help theology hymn God's irreducibility. Indeed, the aesthetic might best suggest God's presence as well as His otherness and might more honestly, albeit obliquely, be the mode through which we experience the God of monotheism.

---

[147] Taylor, pp. 146–147.   [148] Ibid., p. 147, emphasis added.

[149] R. Pannikar, 'Christians and So-Called "Non-Christians"', *CrossCurrents*, vol. 22, no.3 (Summer–Fall 1972), p. 283, emphasis added.

Select Bibliography

Adams, N., Pattison, G., & Ward, G. (eds.), *The Oxford Handbook of Theology and Modern Thought* (Oxford: Oxford University Press, 2013).

Adamson, P., *Philosophy in the Islamic World* (Oxford: Oxford University Press, 2016).

Adorno, T., *The Adorno Reader*, ed. B. O' Connor (Oxford: Blackwell, 2000).

Ali, A. Y. (tr.), *The Holy Qur'an* (Birmingham: Islamic Vision, 1999).

Allison, H. E., *Kant's Theory of Freedom* (Cambridge: Cambridge University Press, 1990).

Alter, R., *Necessary Angels* (Harvard: Harvard University Press, 1991).

Annas, J., *Plato, a Very Short Introduction* (Oxford: Oxford University Press, 2003).

Aquinas, T., *Selected Writings* (London: Penguin Books, 1998).

Aristotle, *Poetics*, tr. M. Heath (London: Penguin Books, 1996).

Arnold, D. W., & Bright, H. (eds.), *De doctrina Christiana: A Classic of Western Culture* (London: University of Notre Dame Press, 1995).

Arnold, J., *Sacred Music in Secular Society* (Farnham: Ashgate, 2014).

Augustine, *Earlier Writings*, tr. John H. S. Burleigh (London: SCM, 'The Library of Christian Classics', vol. vi, 1953).

    Confessions, tr. R. S. Pine-Coffin (London: Penguin Classics, 1961).

    City of God, tr. H. Bettenson (London: Penguin Classics, 1972).

    The Gift of Perseverance, tr. J. A. Mourant, 'The Fathers of the Church', vol. 86 (New York: The Catholic University of America Press, 1992).

    On Free Choice of the Will, tr. T. Williams (Indianapolis, IN: Hackett, 1993).

    De doctrina Christiana, tr. R. P. H. Green (Oxford: Oxford World's Classics, 1997).

    Expositions of the Psalms Volume 4, tr. M. Boulding, 'Augustine for the 21st Century' III/18 (New York: New City Press, 2002).

Ayres, L., & Volpe, M. A. (eds.), *The Oxford Handbook of Catholic Theology* (Oxford: Oxford University Press, 2019).

Barnes, M., *Theology and the Dialogue of Religions* (Cambridge: Cambridge University Press, 2002).

Barth, K., *Protestant Theology in the Nineteenth Century* (London: SCM Press, 2001).

van Beeck, J., *Loving the Torah More than God?* (New York: Loyola University Press, 1989).

Begbie, J., *Voicing Creation's Praise: Towards a Theology of the Arts* (Edinburgh: T & T Clark, 1991).

Theology, Music, and Time (Cambridge: Cambridge University Press, 2000).

Sounding the Depths: Theology through the Arts (Canterbury: SCM, 2002).

Resounding Truth: Christian Wisdom in the World of Music (London: SPCK, 2008).

Begbie, J., *Music, Modernity, and God: Essays in Easy Listening* (Oxford: Oxford University Press, 2013).

A Peculiar Orthodoxy (Ada, MI: Baker Academic, 2018).

Redeeming Transcendence: Bearing Witness to the Triune God (Grand Rapids, MI: Eerdmans, 2018).

Begbie, J., & Guthrie, S. (eds.), *Resonant Witness: Conversations between Music and Theology* (Grand Rapids, MI: Eerdmans, 2011).

Berger, K., *A Theory of Art* (Oxford: Oxford University Press, 2000).

Bach's Cycle, Mozart's Arrow (Berkeley: University of California Press, 2007).

Blackwell, A., *The Sacred in Music* (Cambridge: Lutterworth, 1999).

Bonds, M. E., *Absolute Music: The History of an Idea* (New York: Oxford University Press, 2014).

Bonhoffer, D., *Life Together*, tr. J. W. Doberstein (London: SCM Press, 1954).

Bonner, G., *Augustine* (Norwich: Canterbury Press, 2002).

Bowie, A., *Aesthetics and Subjectivity: From Kant to Nietzsche* (Manchester: Manchester University Press, 1990).

Introduction to German Philosophy from Kant to Habermas (Cambridge: Polity Press, 2003).

Music, Philosophy, and Modernity (Cambridge: Cambridge University Press, 2007).

Bray, K., & Moore, S. D. (eds.), *Religion, Emotion, Sensation: Affect Theories and Theologies* (New York: Fordham University Press, 2020).

Brown, D., *Tradition and Imagination: Revelation and Change* (Oxford: Oxford University Press, 1999).

God and Grace of Body: Sacrament in Ordinary (Oxford: Oxford University Press, 2007).

God and Mystery in Words: Experience through Metaphor and Drama (Oxford: Oxford University Press, 2008).

Brown, J., *Schoenberg and Redemption* (Cambridge: Cambridge University Press, 2014).

Brown, P., *Augustine of Hippo* (London: Faber & Faber, 1967).

Buber, M., *I and Thou*, tr. W. Kaufman (Edinburgh: T & T Clark, 1970).

Buckley, M., *At the Origins of Modern Atheism* (New Haven, CT: Yale University Press, 1987).

Budd, M., *Music and the Emotions, the Philosophical Theories* (London: Routledge, 1985).

Burrell, D. B., *Knowing the Unknowable God: Ibn-Sina, Maimonides, Aquinas* (Notre Dame, IN: University of Notre Dame Press, 1986).

Butt, J. (ed.), *The Cambridge Companion to Bach* (Cambridge: Cambridge University Press, 1997).

  Bach's Dialogue with Modernity: Perspectives on the Passions (Cambridge: Cambridge University Press, 2010).

Campbell, M., & Greated, C., *The Musician's Guide to Acoustics* (New York: Schirmer Books, 1987).

Chadwick, H., *Boethius, the Consolations of Music, Logic, Theology, and Philosophy* (Oxford: Clarendon Press, 1981).

Chamberlain, L., *Nietzsche in Turin* (London: Quartet Books, 1996).

Chua, D., *Absolute Music and the Construction of Meaning* (Cambridge: Cambridge University Press, 1999).

Condillac, E., *Essay on the Origin of Human Knowledge*, tr. H Aarsleff (Cambridge: Cambridge University Press, 2001).

Conway, E., 'A Constant Word in a Changing World: Recognising and Resolving Tensions and Tendencies in a Postmodern Context', *New Blackfriars*, Vol. 87, No. 1008 (March 2006), pp.110–120.

Cooke, D., *The Language of Music* (Oxford: Oxford University Press, 1959).

Copeland, R. M., 'Stravinsky's Christian Message', *The Musical Quarterly*, Vol. 68, No.4 (October 1982), pp.563–579.

Copleston, F., *Arthur Schopenhauer, Philosopher of Pessimism* (London: Burns, Oates & Washbourne, 1946).

  A History of Philosophy, vol. vii (London: Burns & Oates, 1963).

Corbett, G. (ed.), *Annunciations: Sacred Music for the Twenty-First Century* (Cambridge: Open Book, 2019).

Critchley, S., & Bernasconi, R. (eds.), *The Cambridge Companion to Levinas* (Cambridge: Cambridge University Press, 2002).

Dahlhaus, C., *Between Romanticism and Modernism*, tr. M. Whittall (Los Angeles: University of California Press, 1974).

  Esthetics of Music, tr. W. Austin (Cambridge: Cambridge University Press, 1982).

  Schoenberg and the New Music, tr. D. Puffett, & A. Clayton (Cambridge: Cambridge University Press, 1987).

  The Idea of Absolute Music (Chicago, IL: University of Chicago Press, 1989).

Nineteenth-Century Music, tr. J. B. Robinson (Los Angeles: University of California Press, 1989).

Deathridge, J., *Wagner beyond Good and Evil* (Los Angeles: University of California Press, 2008).

Descartes, R., *A Discourse on the Method*, tr. I. Maclean (Oxford: Oxford University Press, 2006).

   Meditations on First Philosophy, tr. M. Moriarty (Oxford: Oxford University Press, 2008).

   The Passions of the Soul, tr. M. Moriarty (Oxford: Oxford University Press, 2015).

Eaghll, T., *From Pietism to Romanticism: The Early Life and Work of Friedrich Schleiermacher*, https://academia.edu/1788694/From Pietism To Romanticism The Early Life and Work of Friedrich Schleiermacher.

Eliot, T. S., *The Sacred Wood: Essays on Poetry and Criticism* (London: Faber & Faber, 1997).

al Faruqi, L. I., 'Music, Musicians, and Muslim Law', *Asian Music*, Autumn – Winter, 1985, Vol. 17, No. 1 (Autumn – Winter, 1985), pp.3–36, University of Texas Press, www.jstor.org/stable/833739.

Feuerbach, L., *The Essence of Christianity*, tr. G. Eliot (New York: Dover, 2008).

Firestone, C. L., & Jacobs, N., *In Defense of Kant's Religion* (Bloomington: Indiana University Press, 2008).

Fitzgerald, A. D., *Augustine through the Ages* (Grand Rapids, MI: Eerdmans, 1999).

Fitzgerald, S. (ed.), *Letters of Flannery O'Connor: The Habit of Being* (New York: Farrar, Strauss & Giroux, 1979).

Forster, M., 'Friedrich Daniel Ernst Schleiermacher', *The Stanford Encyclopedia of Philosophy* (2017 ed.), Edward N. Zalta (ed.), https://plato.stanford.edu/entries/schleiermacher/.

Fosse, J., *A New Name* (London: Fitzcarraldo Editions, 2021).

Gallagher, M., *What Are They Saying about Unbelief?* (New York: Paulist Press, 1995).

Girard, R., *Violence and the Sacred*, tr. P. Gregory (Baltimore, MD: Johns Hopkins University Press, 1977).

   Things Hidden since the Foundation of the World, tr. S. Bann, & M. Metteer (New York: Continuum, 1987).

   The Scapegoat, tr. Y. Freccero (Baltimore, MD: Johns Hopkins University Press, 1989).

   I See Satan Fall Like Lightning, tr. J. G. Williams (Leominster, MA: Gracewing, 2001).

Goldstein, B., *Reinscribing Moses* (Cambridge, MA: Harvard University Press, 1992).

Graham, G., *Philosophy of the Arts: An Introduction to Aesthetics* (Oxon: Routledge, 1983).

The Re-enchantment of the World: Art versus Religion (Oxford: Oxford University Press, 2007).

Gregg, M., & Seigworth, G. J., *The Affect Theory Reader* (Durham, NC: Duke University Press, 2010).

Guite, M., *Faith, Hope, and Poetry: Theology and the Poetic Imagination* (Farnham: Ashgate, 2010).

Gustafson, H., *Finding All Things in God: Pansacramentalism and Doing Theology Interreligiously* (Cambridge: The Lutterworth Press, 2016).

Guyer, P. (ed.), *The Cambridge Companion to Kant* (Cambridge: Cambridge University Press, 1992).

Halim, S. A., *Music & Islam* (Dhaka: Islamic Information Bureau Bangladesh, 2017).

Hamilton, A., *Aesthetics and Music* (London: Continuum, 2007).

Hannay, A., & Marino, G. D. (eds.), *The Cambridge Companion to Kierkegaard* (Cambridge: Cambridge University Press, 1998).

Hanslick, E., *On the Musically Beautiful*, tr. G. Payzant (Indianapolis, IN: Hackett, 1986).

Hare, J. E., *The Moral Gap: Kantian Ethics, Human Limits, and God's Assistance* (Oxford: Oxford University Press, 1996).

Harris, R., & Stokes, M., *Theory and Practice in the Music of the Islamic World: Essays in Honour of Owen Wright* (Abingdon: Routledge, 2019).

Hart, D. B., *The Beauty of the Infinite* (Grand Rapids, MI: Eerdmans, 2003).

Atheist Delusions: The Christian Revolution and Its Fashionable Enemies (New Haven, CT: Yale University Press, 2010).

The Experience of God (New Haven, CT: Yale University Press, 2013).

Theological Territories: A David Bentley Hart Digest (Notre Dame, IN: University of Notre Dame Press, 2020).

Hawkey, J., Quash, B., & White, V. (eds.), *God's Song and Music's Meanings: Theology, Liturgy, and Musicology in Dialogue* (Oxon: Routledge, 2020).

Hesse, H., *Gertrude*, tr. H. Rosner (London: Peter Owens, 1955).

Hewer, C. T. R., *Understanding Islam: The First Ten Steps* (London: SCM Press, 2006).

Hoeckner, B., *Programming the Absolute: Nineteenth-Century German Music and the Hermeneutics of the Moment* (Princeton, NJ: Princeton University Press, 2002).

Charlton, D. (ed.), *E. T. A. Hoffmann's Musical Writings: Kreisleriana, the Poet and the Composer, Music Criticism*, tr. M. Clarke (Cambridge: Cambridge University Press, 1989).

Holness, L., & Wüstenberg, R. K. (eds.), *Theology in Dialogue: The Impact of the Arts, Humanities, and Science on Contemporary Religious Thought* (Grand Rapids, MI: Eerdmans, 2002).

Hopkins, G. M., *Poems and Prose* (London: Penguin, 1985).

Hugues, G. (ed.), *The Philosophical Assessment of Theology: Essays in Honour of Frederick Copleston* (Washington, DC: Georgetown University Press, 1987).

The Nature of God (London: Routledge, 1995).

Ibrahim, C., *Islam and Monotheism* (Cambridge: Cambridge University Press, 2022).

Irving, D., 'Psalms, Islam, and Music: Dialogues and Divergence about David in Christian-Muslim Encounters of the Seventeenth Century', *Yale Journal of Music & Religion*, Vol. 2, No. 1, Article 3 (2016), pp.53–78. https://doi.org/10.17132/2377-231X.1040.

Jacquette, D. (ed.), *Schopenhauer, Philosophy, and the Arts* (Cambridge: Cambridge University Press, 1996).

Janaway, C. (ed.), *The Cambridge Companion to Schopenhauer* (Cambridge: Cambridge University Press, 1999).

Schopenhauer, a Very Short Introduction (Oxford: Oxford University Press, 2002).

Beyond Selflessness (Oxford: Oxford University Press, 2007).

Johnson, J., *Out of Time: Music and the Making of Modernity* (Oxford: Oxford University Press, 2015).

After Debussy: Music, Language, and the Margins of Philosophy (Oxford: Oxford University Press, 2020).

Jones, D., *Epoch and Artist: Selected Writings* (London: Faber and Faber, 1959).

In Parenthesis (London: Faber and Faber, 1961).

The Sleeping Lord: And Other Fragments (London: Faber and Faber, 1974).

Junhof, P., & Biallowons, H. (eds.), *Karl Rahner in Dialogue: Conversations and Interviews* (New York: Crossroad, 1986).

Juslin, P. N., & Sloboda, J. A. (eds.), *Handbook of Music & Emotion: Theory, Research, Applications* (Oxford: Oxford University Press, 2010).

Kant, I., *Religion within the Limits of Reason Alone*, tr. T. M. Greene, & H. H. Hudson (New York: Harper & Row, 1960).

Critique of Practical Reason, tr. T. K. Abbott (New York: Prometheus Books, 1996).

Critique of Pure Reason, tr. M. Weigelt (London: Penguin Classics, 2007).

Groundwork of the Metaphysics of Morals, tr. M. Gregor (Cambridge: Cambridge University Press, 2010).

Kenny, A., *A New History of Western Philosophy* (Oxford: Oxford University Press, 2010).

Khan, H. I., *The Mysticism of Sound and Music: The Sufi Teaching of Hazrat Inayat Khan* (Boulder, CO: Shambhala, 1991).

Kierkegaard, S., *Fear and Trembling*, tr. A. Hannay (London: Penguin Classics, 1985).

Either/Or, tr. A. Hannay (London: Penguin Classics, 1992).

Kilby, K., *Karl Rahner* (London: Fount, 1997).

Knox, F. B., & Lonsdale, D., *Poetry and the Religious Imagination: The Power of the Word* (Abingdon: Routledge, 2016).

Lash, N., *Theology on Dover Beach* (Eugene, OR: Wipf & Stock, 1979).

Theology on the Way to Emmaus (Eugene, OR: Wipf & Stock, 1986).

Easter in Ordinary: Reflections on Human Experience and the Knowledge of God (London: SCM Press, 1988).

Theology for Pilgrims (London: DLT, 2008).

Fourth Lateran Council of 1215, https://documentacatholicaomnia.eu/03d/ 1215-1215,_Concilium_Lateranum_IIII,_Documenta_Omnia,_EN.pdf.

Latour, B., 'How to Talk About the Body? The Normative Dimension of Science Studies', www.bruno-latour.fr/sites/default/files/77-BODY-NORMATIVE-BS-GB.pdf.

Layton, R. (ed.), *A Guide to the Symphony* (Oxford: Oxford University Press, 1995).

Van Leeuwen, M. T., 'Text, Canon, and Revelation in Paul Ricoeur's Hermeneutics', https://brill.com/previewpdf/book/edcoll/9789004379060/ B9789004379060_s029.xml.

Levinas, E., *Collected Philosophical Papers* (Pittsburgh, PA: Duquesne University Press, 1987).

The Levinas Reader (Oxford: Blackwell, 1989).

Difficult Freedom: Essays on Judaism (Baltimore, MD: John Hopkins University Press, 1990).

Beyond the Verse (London: Continuum, 1994).

Entre Nous (London: Continuum, 1998).

In the Time of the Nations (London: Continuum, 2007).

Lewisohn, L., 'The Sacred Music of Islam: Samā' in the Persian Sufi Tradition', *British Journal of Ethnomusicology*, Vol. 6 (1997), pp.1–33.

Lippitt, J., & Urpeth, J. (eds.), *Nietzsche and the Divine* (Manchester: Clinamen Press, 2000).

Lochhead, L., *A Choosing: The Selected Poems of Liz Lochhead* (Edinburgh: Polygon, 2011).

Lodes, B., 'When I Try, Now and Then, to Give Musical Form to My Turbulent Feelings: The Human and the Divine in the Gloria of Beethoven's *Missa Solemnis*', *Beethoven Forum 6*, Lincoln, Nebraska University Press (1998).

Loos, A., 'Art & Architecture', www.google.co.uk/search?q=Adolf+Loos+archi tecture+images&biw=1920&bih=960&tbm=isch&tbo=u&source= univ&sa=X&ved=0ahUKEwi5t87Uj5nQAhVLI8AKHRgABQIQsAQII Q#imgrc=_.

Lossky, V., *The Mystical Theology of the Eastern Church* (Cambridge: James Clarke, 1957).

de Lubac, H., *The Drama of Atheist Humanism* (San Francisco, CA: Ignatius Press, 1949).

MacCulloch, D., *Reformation: Europe's House Divided 1490–1700* (London: Penguin, 2003).

MacSwain, R., & Taylor, W. (eds.), *Theology, Aesthetics, and Culture: Responses to the Work of David Brown* (Oxford: Oxford University Press, 2012).

Magee, B., *The Philosophy of Schopenhauer* (Oxford: Oxford University Press, 1983).

Wagner and Philosophy (London: Penguin Books, 2000).

Magnus, B., & Higgins K. M. (eds.), *The Cambridge Companion to Nietzsche* (Cambridge: Cambridge University Press, 1996).

Mann, T., *Buddenbrooks*, tr. H. T. Lowe-Porter (London: Vintage, 1924).

Doctor Faustus, tr. H. T. Lowe-Porter (London: Vintage, 1949).

The Magic Mountain, tr. H. T. Lowe-Porter (London: Vintage, 1952).

Death in Venice and Other Stories, tr. D. Lurke (London: Vintage, 1988).

Mariña, J., 'Kant on Grace: A Reply to His Critics', *Religious Studies*, Vol. 33 (1997), pp.379–400.

(ed.), *The Cambridge Companion to Friedrich Schleiermacher* (Cambridge: Cambridge University Press, 2005).

Marissen, M., *Lutheranism, Anti-Judaism, and Bach's St John Passion* (Oxford: Oxford University Press, 1998).

Maritain, J., *Art and Scholasticism*, tr. B. Barbour (Tacoma, WA: Cluny Media, 2016).

Marmion, D., & Hines, M. E. (eds.), *The Cambridge Companion to Karl Rahner* (Cambridge: Cambridge University Press, 2006).

Marsh, C., & Roberts, V. S., *Personal Jesus: How Popular Music Shapes Our Souls* (Grand Rapids, MI: Baker Academic, 2012).

McDade, J., 'The Trinity and the Paschal Mystery', *Heythrop Journal*, Vol. xxix (1988), pp.175–191.

Mellers, W., *Bach and the Dance of God* (London: Faber & Faber, 1980).
Beethoven and the Voice of God (London: Faber & Faber, 1983).

Mezei, B., 'The Sovereignty of Revelation: On Paul Ricoeur's Hermeneutics of Revelation', https://journals.sagepub.com/doi/10.1177/00084298211 044814.

Michalson, G., *Fallen Freedom* (Cambridge: Cambridge University Press, 1990).

Miel, J., *Pascal and Theology* (Baltimore, MD: Johns Hopkins Press, 1969).

Milosz, C., *To Begin Where I Am: Selected Essays* (New York: Farrar, Straus & Giroux, 2001).
Legends of Modernity: Essays and Letters from Occupied Poland, 1942–1943, tr. M. G. Levine (New York: Farrar, Straus & Giroux, 2005).
New and Collected Poems, 1931–2001 (London: Penguin, 2005).
Selected and Last Poems, 1931–2004 (London: Penguin, 2014).

Morgan, M., *Discovering Levinas* (New York: Cambridge University Press, 2007).

Morgan, M., & Gordon, P. E. (eds.), *The Cambridge Companion to Modern Jewish Philosophy* (Cambridge: Cambridge University Press, 2007).

Morrier, D., *Monteverdi: Secondo Libro de Madrigali*, Concerto Italiano, Rinaldo Alessandrini (Opus 111, OPS – 30–111, 1992).

Murdoch, I., *Existentialists and Mystics* (London: Chatto & Windus, 1997).

Nelson, K., *The Art of Reciting the Qur'an* (Austin: University of Texas Press, 1985).

New World Encyclopedia Contributors, 'Emmanuel Levinas', *New World Encyclopedia*, www.newworldencyclopedia.org/entry/Emmanuel_Lévinas.

Nietzsche, F., *The Will to Power*, tr. W. Kaufmann (New York: Vintage Press, 1967).
The Gay Science, tr. W. Kaufmann (New York: Vintage Press, 1974).
Human, All Too Human, tr. M. Faber, & S. Lehmann (London: Penguin Classics, 1984).
The Birth of Tragedy, tr. S. Whiteside (London: Penguin Classics, 1997).
On the Genealogy of Morality, tr. C. Diethe (Cambridge: Cambridge University Press, 1997).
Beyond Good and Evil, tr. R. J. Hollingdale (London: Penguin Classics, 2003).
Thus Spake Zarathustra, tr. R. J. Hollingdale (London: Penguin Classics, 2003).
Twilight of the Idols and *The Anti-Christ*, tr. R. J. Hollingdale (London: Penguin Classics, 2003).
Ecce Homo, tr. R. J. Hollingdale (London: Penguin Classics, 2004).

Daybreak, tr. R. J. Hollingdale (Cambridge: Cambridge University Press, 2009).

Oakes, E. T., & Moss, D. (eds.), *The Cambridge Companion to Hans Urs von Balthasar* (Cambridge: Cambridge University Press, 2004).

O'Connor, B. (ed.), *The Adorno Reader* (Oxford: Blackwell, 2000).

O'Connor, F., *Mystery and Manners* (London: Faber & Faber, 1972).

Owen, D., *Nietzsche's 'Genealogy of Morality'* (Stocksfield: Acumen, 2007).

Pannikar, R., 'Christians and So-Called "Non-Christians"', *CrossCurrents*, Vol. 22, No.3 (1972), pp.281–308.

Partridge, C., *The Lyre of Orpheus: Popular Music, the Sacred, & the Profane* (Oxford: Oxford University Press, 2014).

Pascal, B., *Pensées*, tr. A. J. Krailsheimer (London: Penguin Classics, 1966).
  Provincial Letters, tr. A. J. Krailsheimer (London: Penguin Classics, 1967).
  Oeuvres Completes, vol. iii, ed. J. Mesnard (Paris: Desclée de Brouwer, 1991)
  Pensées and Other Writings, tr. H. Levi (Oxford: Oxford University Press, 1995).

Pattison, G., *Kierkegaard: The Aesthetic and the Religious: From the Magic Theatre to the Crucifixion of the Image* (New York: St Martin's Press, 1992).
  Kierkegaard's Theory and Critique of Art: Its Theological Significance http://etheses.dur.ac.uk/7823/7823_4820.PDF?UkUDh:CyT.

Pekarske, D., *Abstracts of Karl Rahner's Theological Investigations 1-23* (Milwaukee, WI: Marquette University Press, 2002).

Pelagius, *The Letters of Pelagius and His Followers*, ed. B. R. Rees (Woodbridge: Boydell Press, 1991).

Pelikan, J., *Bach among the Theologians* (Eugene, OR: Wipf & Stock, 1986).

Perlmutter, J., *Sacred Music, Religious Desire and Knowledge of God: The Music of Our Human Longing* (London: Bloomsbury Academic, 2020).

Plato, *Laws*, tr. T. J. Saunders (London: Penguin Classics, 1970).
  The Republic, tr. D. Lee (London: Penguin Classics, 2007).
  Timaeus and Critias, tr. D. Lee (London: Penguin Books, 2008).

Potok, C., *My Name Is Asher Lev* (London: Penguin Books, 1973).

Potok, C., *The Gift of Asher Lev* (New York: Fawcett Books, 1990).

Pott, F., *Mäntyjärvi: Choral Music*, CD booklet notes (London: Hyperion, 2020).

Pseudo-Dionysius, *The Complete Works*, tr. C. Luibheid (New York: Paulist Press, 1987).

Quash, B., *Found Theology: History, Imagination and the Holy Spirit* (London: Bloomsbury T & T Clark, 2013).

Rahner, K., *Theological Investigations*, vol. 4 (London: DLT, 1966).

Theological Investigations, vol. 5 (London: DLT, 1966).

Foundations of the Christian Faith (London: DLT, 1978).

Theological Investigations, vol. 23 (London: DLT, 1992).

The Content of Faith (New York: Crossroad, 1999).

Rameau, J., *Treatise on Harmony*, tr. P. Gossett (New York: Dover, 1971).

Regan, E., *Theology and the Boundary Discourse of Human Rights* (Washington, DC: Georgetown University Press, 2010).

Ricoeur, P., *Essays on Biblical Interpretation*, ed. L. S. Mudge (London: Fortress Press, 1980).

Robbins, J., *Altered Reading: Levinas and Literature* (Chicago, IL: Chicago University Press, 1999).

Robertson, R. (ed.), *The Cambridge Companion to Thomas Mann* (Cambridge: Cambridge University Press, 2006).

Rolland, R., *Jean-Christophe, Journey's End: Love and Friendship, the Burning Bush, the New Dawn*, tr. G. Cannan (Milton Keynes: Wildside, 1913).

Rousseau, J. J., *Essay on the Origin of Languages*, tr. J. H. Moran (Chicago, IL: Chicago University Press, 1966).

Russell, B., *History of Western Philosophy* (London: Routledge Classics, 2004).

Russill, P., *Stevens: Mass for Double Choir*, The Finzi Singers, Paul Spicer (Chandos, CHAN 9021).

Sacks, J., *The Dignity of Difference: How to Avoid the Clash of Civilisations* (London: Continuum, 2002).

Covenant & Conversation: Genesis (Jerusalem: Maggid, 2009).

Safranski, R., *Nietzsche, a Philosophical Biography*, tr. S. Frisch (London: Granta Books, 2003).

Saliers, D., *Music and Theology* (Nashville, TN: Abingdon Press, 2007).

Schleiermacher, F., *On Religion: Speeches to Its Cultured Despisers*, tr. R. Crouter (Cambridge: Cambridge University Press, 2008).

Schoenberg, A., *Theory of Harmony*, tr. R. E. Carter (London: Faber & Faber, 1922).

Structural Function of Harmony (New York: Norton, 1954).

Letters, ed. E. Stein (London: Faber & Faber, 1964).

Fundamentals of Musical Composition (London: Faber & Faber, 1967).

Style & Idea: Selected Writings of Arnold Schoenberg, tr. L. Black (London: Faber & Faber, 1975).

'Eine Unterredung vor Zugasbang', www.schoenberg.at/index.php/en/bei-arnold-schoenberg-eine-unterredung-vor-zugsabang-2.

Scholem, G., *Major Trends in Jewish Mysticism* (New York: Schocken Books, 1974).

Schopenhauer, A., *On the Basis of Morality*, tr. E. F. J. Payne (New York: Bobbs-Merrill, 1965).

World as Will and Representation, vols. I & II, tr. E. F. J. Payne (New York: Dover, 1969).

Prize Essay on the Freedom of the Will, tr. E. F. J. Payne (Cambridge: Cambridge University Press, 1999).

Essays and Aphorisms, tr. R. J. Hollingdale (London: Penguin Classics, 2004).

Schwager, R., *Must There Be Scapegoats?: Violence and Redemption in the Bible*, tr. M. L. Assad (San Francisco, CA: Harper & Row, 1987).

Jesus in the Drama of Salvation: Towards a Biblical Doctrine of Redemption, tr. J. G Williams, & P. Haddon (New York: Crossroad, 1999).

Scruton, R., *The Aesthetics of Music* (Oxford: Oxford University Press, 1997).

Death-Devoted Heart: Sex and the Sacred in Wagner's Tristan and Isolde (Oxford: Oxford University Press, 2004).

Effing the Ineffable – Sir Roger Scruton (roger-scruton.com).

Shantz, D., *An Introduction to German Pietism: Protestant Renewal at the Dawn of Modern Europe* (Baltimore, MD: Johns Hopkins University Press, 2013).

Shaw, J., & Auner, J. (eds.), *The Cambridge Companion to Schoenberg* (Cambridge: Cambridge University Press, 2010).

Shiloah, A., 'Music and Religion in Islam', *Acta Musicologica*, Vol. 69, Fasc. 2 (July–December, 1997), pp.143–155, cf. p.143. Published by: International Musicological Society, www.jstpr.org/stable/932653.

Smart, N., Clayton, J., Sherry, P., & Katz, S. (eds.), *Nineteenth Century Religious Thought in the West* (Cambridge: Cambridge University Press, 1985).

Solomon, N., *Judaism: A Very Short Introduction* (Cambridge: Cambridge University Press, 2014).

Steiner, G., *Real Presences* (Chicago, IL: Chicago University Press, 1989).

Language and Silence (New Haven, CT: Yale University Press, 1998).

Grammars of Creation (London: Faber & Faber, 2002).

Stone-Davis, F., *Musical Beauty: Negotiating the Boundary between Subject and Object* (La Vergne, TN: Wipf & Stock, 2011).

Stravinsky, I., & Craft, R., *Conversations with Igor Stravinsky* (London: Faber & Faber, 1979).

Dialogues (London: Faber & Faber, 1982).

Stump, E., & Kretzmann, N. (eds.), *The Cambridge Companion to Augustine* (Cambridge: Cambridge University Press, 2001).

Tanner, M., *Nietzsche* (Oxford: Oxford University Press, 1994).

Nietzsche, a Very Short Introduction (Oxford: Oxford University Press, 1994).

Taruskin, R., 'Art and the Unconscious', www.oxfordwesternmusic.com/view/Volume4/actrade-9780195384840-div1-006004.xml.

Taylor, C., *Sources of the Self: The Making of the Modern Identity* (Cambridge, MA: Harvard University Press, 1989)

A Secular Age (Cambridge, MA: Harvard University Press, 2007).

The Language Animal: The Full Shape of the Human Linguistic Capacity (Cambridge, MA: Belknap Press of Harvard University Press, 2016).

Thiessen, G., *Theological Aesthetics: SCM Reader* (London: SCM Press, 2004).

Thomas, D. A., *Music and the Origins of Language: Theories from the French Enlightenment* (Cambridge: Cambridge University Press, 1995).

Thomas, R. S., *Collected Poems, 1945–1990* (London: Phoenix, 1993).

Ticciati, S., *A New Apophaticism: Augustine and the Redemption of Signs* (Boston, MA: Brill, 2015).

Trier, D. J., Husbands, M., & Lundin, R. (eds.), *The Beauty of God: Theology and the Arts* (Lisle, IL: InterVarsity Press Academic, 2007).

Turner, H. E. W., *Jesus the Christ* (London: Mowbray, 1976).

Vergo, P., *That Divine Order* (London: Phaidon Press, 2005).

Viladesau, R., *Theological Aesthetics: God in Imagination, Beauty, and Art* (New York: Oxford University Press, 1999).

Wackenroder, W. H., *Confessions & Fantasies*, tr. M. H. Schubert (London: Pennsylvania State University Press, 1971).

Wagner, R., *Religion and Art*, tr. W. Ashton Ellis (Lincoln: University of Nebraska Press, 1994).

Jesus of Nazareth and Other Writings, tr. W. Ashton Ellis (Lincoln: University of Nebraska Press, 1995).

Walden, D. (ed.), *Conversations with Chaim Potok* (Jackson: University of Mississippi Press, 2001).

Watkins, H., *Metaphors of Depth in German Musical Thought* (Cambridge: Cambridge University Press, 2011).

Webster, J. (ed.), *The Cambridge Companion to Karl Barth* (Cambridge: Cambridge University Press, 2006).

Wehrs, D. R., & Blake, T. (eds.), *The Palgrave Handbook of Affect Studies and Textual Criticism* (Cham: Palgrave MacMillan, 2017).

Weinandy, T., *Does God Suffer?* (London: University of Notre Dame Press, 1999).

Wendel, F., *Calvin* (London: Collins, 1963).

Williams, J. G. (ed.), *The Girard Reader* (New York: Crossroad, 1996).

Williams, R., *On Christian Theology* (Oxford: Blackwell, 2000).

    Grace and Necessity: Reflections on Art and Love (London: Continuum, 2005).

    Wrestling with Angels: Conversations in Modern Theology (London: SCM Press, 2007).

    Dostoevsky (Waco, TX: Baylor University Press, 2008).

    The Edge of Words: God and the Habits of Language (London: Bloomsbury, 2014).

Wolff, C., *Johann Sebastian Bach: The Learned Musician* (Oxford: Oxford University Press, 2001).

Zarepour, M. S., *Necessary Existence and Monotheism* (Cambridge: Cambridge University Press, 2022).

Acknowledgements

I would like to thank the series editors, Chad Meister and Paul Moser, for the invitation to undertake this project. My former doctoral supervisor, Professor Ben Quash (King's College London), has provided constant encouragement, as has Dr John McDade (former Principal of Heythrop College, London University), to whom I am grateful for introducing me to the novels of Chaim Potok. I am delighted to have made the acquaintance of Jeremy Schonfield and Gershon Silins, who have welcomed this project and have been generous with their information.

The choirs of Christ Church, Chelsea, and the Chapel Choir of Girton College, Cambridge, have been willing participants and, more often than not, guides in my musical/liturgical journey, while the support of my own family, Tom, Phyllis, Julie, Jenni, Laurence, Lea, Josiah, Esther, and Kamran has been a source of strength on numerous occasions. Holly Slater's unfailing support remains as precious now as when we first met.

As the final stages of this project were reached, in April 2023, followers of Abrahamic faiths the world over simultaneously celebrated Passover, Easter, and Ramadan, an overlapping which occurs only three times per century. While the celebration of Holy Week in solidarity with millions of other Christians is special enough, there was something quite magical about knowing that billions of people the world over were united in concentrated worship of the one God whose communication to us takes the form of connecting us despite our differences.

Lastly, I would like to pay tribute to my musical mentor and close friend, George Taylor FRSAMD (1934–2022). A man of genius and a man of faith, his recent passing would constitute the most painful absence were he not still so very present. This book is dedicated to him.

Cambridge Elements ≡

Religion and Monotheism

Elements in the Series

A full series listing is available at: www.cambridge.org/er&m

Printed in the United States
by Baker & Taylor Publisher Services